BUILDING CLASSROOM DISCIPLINE

Third Edition

C. M. Charles
San Diego State University

Collaboration by

Karen Blaine Barr

Longman
New York & London

Building Classroom Discipline, 3rd edition

Longman, 95 Church Street, White Plains, N. Y. 10601

Associated companies:
Longman Group Ltd., London
Longman Cheshire Pty., Melbourne
Longman Paul Pty., Auckland
Copp Clark Pitman, Toronto
Pitman Publishing Inc., New York

p. 40 photo credit: Harvard University News Office
p. 55 photo credit: AP/World Wide Photos
p. 69 photo credit: Alfred Adler Institute of Chicago
p. 118 photo credit: Honolulu Star Bulletin

Executive editor: Ray O'Connell
Production editor: Camilla T. K. Palmer
Text design: Lynn Luchetti
Cover design: Steven Krastin
Photo research: Marty Levick
Production supervisor: Judy Stern

Library of Congress Cataloging-in-Publication Data
Charles, C. M.
    Building classroom discipline.
    Includes bibliographies and index.
    1. School discipline. 2. Classroom management.
I. Barr, Karen Blaine. II. Title.
LB3012.C46 1989   371.5   88-6777

ISBN 0-8013-0230-7
DEFGHIJ-DO-959493929190

Contents

Introduction

The scene is an inner-city school. Classroom 314 is quiet as students listen attentively to the teacher's questions about a recent lesson. Suddenly, eager hands begin to wave and bodies twist out of their seats amidst shouts of "ooh me," "I know," "ooh-oh." Quiet returns when one student is chosen to answer. As soon as she has responded, others begin to yell out refutations or additions and compete again for teacher recognition. As they participate wholeheartedly in class, several students are simultaneously but secretly passing notes and candy and signaling to each other in sign and face language. When the questions end and seat work begins, some students offer to help others who are unsure of how to proceed.

But across the hall in room 315, chaos reigns. The room is noisy with the shouting, laughter, and movement of many children. Though most students are seated, many are walking or running aimlessly around the classroom. Some stop at others' desks, provoke them briefly, and move on. Several students who are lining up textbooks as "race courses" for toy cars laugh when the teacher demands their attention. As the teacher struggles to ask a question over the noise, few if any students volunteer to answer. When one student does respond correctly, others yell out "You think you're so smart." (Schwartz, 1981)

By most teachers' standards, the discipline in Classroom 314 is good, while that in Classroom 315 is poor. But what is the difference? In both rooms students are making noise and doing things they are not supposed to do. Yet the teacher in 314 is probably quite satisfied with the lesson while the teacher in 315 is probably frustrated and laboring with stress. Why?

One purpose of this book is to help you find a clear answer to that question, but first it is necessary to distinguish between acceptable classroom behavior and unacceptable behavior—what is referred to as misbehavior. That distinction is explained as follows:

BEHAVIOR AND MISBEHAVIOR

Behavior is defined as all the physical and mental acts that humans perform. Thus, behavior is whatever one does, whether good or bad, right or wrong, helpful or useless, productive or wasteful. In contrast *misbehavior* is a label applied to any behavior that is considered to be inappropriate to the setting or situation in which it occurs. Most classroom misbehavior is considered to be done intentionally by students, when they know they should not do it. An inadvertent hiccup during quiet work time is not misbehavior, but when feigned for the purpose of disrupting a lesson the same behavior is justifiably disapproved by the teacher.

Five Types of Misbehavior

Teachers contend with five broad types of misbehavior. In order of seriousness, as judged by social scientists, they are:

1. *Aggression*, physical and verbal attacks by students on the teacher or other students.
2. *Immorality*, acts such as cheating, lying, and stealing.
3. *Defiance of authority*, where students refuse, sometimes hostilely, to do what the teacher tells them to do.
4. *Class disruptions*, such as talking loudly, calling out, walking about the room, clowning, tossing objects, and so forth. (Most class behavior rules focus on this category of misbehavior.)
5. *Goofing off*, fooling around, not doing the assigned tasks, daydreaming, and so forth.

Teachers agree with the levels of social seriousness shown here for the five categories of misbehavior. Indeed, they are very concerned about aggression, immorality, and defiance and dread having to deal with them. But in practice, the amount of time and energy expended on dealing with misbehaviors, even in the urban classrooms typically seen as more problematic, is heavily weighted toward the less serious actions, such as goofing off and disrupting.

In a sense, then, the less nocuous behaviors are the more serious for teachers, because they waste instructional time and interfere with learning. And precisely because they regard them as less serious, teachers are often less confident or aggressive in responding to them. Lee Canter, whose Assertive Discipline is one of the most widely-used discipline systems, was asked how he could justify sending a student to the office for a misbehavior as mild as (repeatedly) talking without permission. He replied that it was precisely such behaviors, which no one considers *that* bad, that drive teachers crazy because they so strongly interfere with teaching and learning.

DISCIPLINE AND MISBEHAVIOR

The word discipline has several different meanings, but throughout this book it is used to refer to steps taken to cause students to behave acceptably in school. Discipline is tied directly to misbehavior—where there is no misbehavior, no discipline is required. Teachers dream of such classes but rarely encounter them.

Discipline is intended to suppress, control, and redirect misbehavior —behavior that is aggressive, immoral, or disruptive to learning. All teachers know that students sometimes behave with sweetness, kindness, gentility, consideration, helpfulness, and honesty. That makes teaching one of the most satisfying and rewarding of all professions. But teachers also know, though they fervently wish it weren't so, that students sometimes behave with hostility, abusiveness, disrespect, disinterest, and cruelty—all of which reduce effectiveness of and pleasure in teaching and learning.

IS DISCIPLINE ALL THAT SERIOUS?

Some teachers have virtually no discipline problems, and they can't see why others should have them. Discipline is really not such a big deal, they say. Teachers in training often have the idea that students are inherently kind, and that if you treat them with kindness and respect they will treat you and other students the same way. Are the horror stories about discipline warranted? Is discipline really such a serious matter? Judge for yourself.

Each year since 1969 Phi Delta Kappa has sponsored a Gallup Poll of the public's attitudes toward education. One question on the survey asks: "What do you think are the biggest problems with which the public schools in this community must contend?" In the vast majority of the years since 1969, the public has listed discipline as the number one problem. Although on occasion other concerns have been placed in the number one position, overall no other concern has come close to that of discipline (Gallup and Clark, 1987).

Let it be recognized that public opinion can be suspect because it is so influenced by the sensational—things such as physical attacks on teachers and severe vandalism of schools. In the case of discipline, however, one hears little disagreement with the view held by the public. In general, both teachers and students are highly concerned about discipline. In the 1981 Nationwide Teacher Opinion Poll conducted by the National Education Association, 9 teachers in 10 said that student misbehavior interfered with their teaching, and 25% of them said it interfered greatly. That report also revealed that 110,000 teachers suffered physical attacks from students during the previous 12 months, most of them in the classroom. One-third of the teachers said they were sometimes or often afraid of personal attack from students ("Opinion Poll," 1981a).

The situation has not improved. In 1987 the California Department of Education released statistics indicating that during the previous year there were 162,700 reported incidents of crime and violence in California public schools. The majority were crimes against property, but 74,400 of them were incidents of assault on students, teachers, and other school personnel.

In 1981 Donald Cruickshank reported a 15-year study of problems that interfere with teachers' ability to teach. Prominent among the five problem areas identified was one that Cruickshank called "control." He explained that "Teachers want pupils to behave appropriately—to be relatively quiet, orderly, and courteous. They also expect students to be honest and to show respect for others and for property" (p. 403).

Difficulty with class control is acknowledged to produce exceptionally high levels of stress in teachers, levels so severe that they have been likened to the battle fatigue experienced by soldiers in combat. Symptoms of this stress include exhaustion, frustration, tension, high blood pressure, severe depression, and alcoholism ("Trends," 1981b)

The concern about discipline is not waning; rather, it is growing stronger. Numerous recent studies have listed discipline as one of the major problems with which teachers must contend and a major factor in the high numbers of teachers leaving the profession—now 40% departure during teachers' first 3 years ("Study Backs," 1987). Adding to the problem is that experienced teachers move away, if possible, from schools with especially difficult discipline situations, leaving those schools to beginning teachers who are not yet adept in dealing with misbehavior (Brooks, 1987). In an effort to deal with the problem, both teacher training programs and inservice programs for beginning teachers are giving increased emphasis to practical techniques of discipline and classroom management.

THE INTENT AND ORGANIZATION OF THIS BOOK

The primary purpose of this book is to help you develop practical skills for organizing and maintaining effective discipline in your classroom. Ultimately you must give strong attention to three aspects of discipline, which are labeled:

- *Preventive Discipline*—referring to what you can do to prevent misbehavior from occurring in the first place.
- *Supportive Discipline*—referring to what you can do to assist students when they show first signs of incipient misbehavior.
- *Corrective Discipline*—referring to what you can do to suppress and positively redirect misbehavior once it does occur.

You must organize these three facets of discipline into a coordinated system, which is understood and accepted by your students and which you can implement and enforce humanely and positively.

The information, activities, and suggestions presented in the following chapters will enable you to organize and implement an effective system of your own, one that matches your philosophy, personality, and teaching realities. It is much more likely that such a system will work for you, than will a ready-made system you adopt from elsewhere and try to implement in your classroom.

The book is organized to guide you through the following experiences: First, you will examine elements of eight important and established systems of discipline. Referred to as "models of discipline," they have historical, theoretical, and/or practical value. Some are widely used today, and all can contribute to your thinking about discipline.

Next, you will encounter chapters that supplement the models by adding information and further suggestions that you will find useful when formulating a personal system of discipline.

Finally, you will see guidelines for use in building your own personal system of discipline, followed by illustrative examples of discipline systems organized and implemented by teachers at various grade levels.

REFERENCES

Brooks, D. (Ed.). (1987). Teacher induction: a new beginning. Reston, VA:Association of Teacher Educators.

Canter, L. (1979). "Assertive Discipline." Audio tape. Alexandria, VA: Association for Supervision and Curriculum Development.

Cruickshank, D. (1981). What we know about teachers' problems, *Educational Leadership, 38*, 402–405.

Gallup, A., & Clark, D. (1987). The 19th annual Gallup poll of the public's attitudes toward the public schools. *Phi Delta Kappan, 69 (No. 1)*, 17–30.

Opinion poll: disruptive behavior. (1981a). *Today's education*, 70, 10.

Schwartz, F. (1981). Supporting or subverting learning: peer group patterns in four tracked schools. *Anthropology and Education Quarterly, 12 (No. 2)*, 99–120.

Study backs induction schools to help new teachers stay teachers. (1987). *ASCD Update, 29 (No. 4)*, 1.

Trends: teachers suffer stress around the world. (1981b). *Today's Education*, 70, 6.

PART ONE
Eight Models of Discipline

CHAPTER 1

The Redl and Wattenberg Model:

Dealing with the Group

REDL AND WATTENBERG
BIOGRAPHICAL SKETCHES

Fritz Redl immigrated to the United States from Austria in 1936. He worked as a therapist, researcher, and professor of behavioral science at Wayne State University. In 1973 he became a consultant to the department of criminal justice at State University of New York at Albany, dealing with deviant juveniles. His writings in the field of education consist of *Mental Hygiene in Teaching*, co-authored with William Wattenberg (1951), *Discipline for Today's Children*, co-authored with George Sheviakov (1956), and *When We Deal with Children* (1972).

William W. Wattenberg, born in 1911, received his PhD degree from Columbia University in 1936. He specialized in educational psychology, which he has taught at Northwestern University, Chicago Teacher's College, and Wayne State University. Dr. Wattenberg's writings include *Mental Hygiene in Teaching*, co-authored with Fritz Redl (1951), *The Adolescent Years* (1955), and *All Men Are Created Equal* (1967).

In their book *Mental Hygiene in Teaching*, Redl and Wattenberg provided insights into the forces—psychological and social—that affect student behavior in classroom groups. They were among the first to offer teachers specific disciplinary techniques that can be used in every-day situations—techniques designed to maintain classroom control and strengthen emotional development in students.

REDL AND WATTENBERG'S CENTRAL FOCUS

Group behavior differs from individual behavior. Teachers can learn how to use influence techniques to deal with undesirable aspects of group behavior.

Redl and Wattenberg's Key Ideas

1. People in groups behave differently than they do individually. Group expectations influence individual behavior, and individual behavior affects the group. Teachers need to be aware of the characteristic traits of group behavior.
2. Groups create their own psychological forces that influence individual behavior. Teacher awareness of *group dynamics* is important to effective classroom control.
3. Group behavior in the classroom is influenced by how students perceive the teacher. Students see teachers as filling many psychological roles.

4. Dealing with classroom conflict requires diagnostic thinking by the teacher. This thinking involves: (1) forming a first hunch, (2) gathering facts, (3) applying hidden factors, (4) taking action, and (5) being flexible.

5. Teachers maintain group control through various *influence techniques.* These techniques include: (1) supporting self-control, (2) offering situational assistance, (3) appraising reality, and (4) invoking pleasure and pain.

6. *Supporting self-control techniques* are low keyed. They address the problem before it becomes serious. They include eye contact, moving closer, encouragement, humor, and ignoring.

7. *Situational assistance* techniques are necessary when students cannot regain control without assistance from the teacher. Techniques to provide assistance include: (1) helping students over a hurdle, (2) restructuring the schedule, (3) establishing routines, (4) removing the student from a situation, (5) removing seductive objects, and (6) physical restraint.

8. *Appraising reality* techniques involve helping students understand underlying causes for misbehavior and foresee probable consequences. Teachers "tell it like it is," offer encouragement, set limits, and clarify situations with post-situational follow-up.

9. *Pleasure-pain* techniques involve rewarding good behavior and punishing bad behavior. Punishment should be used only as a last resort because it is too often counterproductive.

GROUP LIFE IN THE CLASSROOM

Understanding motivations, the basic causes behind behavior and conflict, is half the battle of classroom control. Our knowledge of individual behavior is growing daily. Teachers know better than ever before why individuals behave as they do, and that outward behavior has roots in identifiable needs. They know that students are continually torn between personal desires and expectations of society.

However, teachers seldom deal with students on a purely individual basis. Instead, they must concern themselves with groups—the entire class, large groups, and smaller groups. This does not mean that they cannot use their valuable insights into individual behavior, but that they must instead transfer those insights into group behavior. This presents a major problem: group psychology is different from individual psychology. People simply behave differently when in groups.

Redl and Wattenberg view the group as an organism. "A group creates conditions such that its members will behave in certain ways because they belong to it; at the same time, the manner in which the parts function affects the whole" (Redl and Wattenberg 1959, p. 267). In other words, group expectations strongly influence individual behavior, and individual behavior in turn affects the group. Redl and Wattenberg describe several roles that are available to individuals in groups. The following are some of the roles that can cause trouble in the classroom.

Leader

A leadership role is available in almost every group. The role varies according to the group's purpose, makeup, and activities. Within the same group, different people may act as leaders in different activities. For example, a student who is a leader in physical education may fill a different role in music.

Group leaders tend to share certain qualities. They are above average in most respects (intellect, responsibility, social skills, and socioeconomic status). They generally have a highly developed understanding of others, and they embody group ideals.

Teachers must be aware that the leaders they appoint are not necessarily the group's natural leaders. Such mismatches often lead to conflict within the group.

Clowns

Clowns are individuals who take the position of entertainer in the group. Students sometimes take this role in order to mask feelings of inferiority, thinking it best to make fun of themselves before others have a chance. Clowns sometimes help the group and sometimes hinder it. Clowning can be beneficial to both teacher and the group, especially when students are anxious, frustrated, or in need of relief from tension. At times, however, group members may support the disruptive antics of the clown as a way of expressing hostility to the teacher.

Fall Guys

A fall guy is an individual who takes blame and punishment in order to gain favor with the group. Members of the group feel free to misbehave knowing that they can set up the fall guy to suffer the penalties. Teachers need to be aware of this kind of manipulation and be sure to focus their corrective actions on the instigators of misbehavior.

Instigators

Instigators are individuals who cause trouble, but appear not to be involved. They often solve their inner conflicts by getting others to act them out. They may even feel that they are benefiting the victim in some way. Teachers need to look into recurring conflicts carefully to see if there is an unnoticed instigator. It may be necessary to point out this role to the group, as it is often undetected by them. The group may need help in recognizing and discouraging this role.

Comment on Group Roles

All of the roles described here are played by individuals in groups either because the role fills a strong personal need or because the group expects or enjoys it. By playing a role, an individual finds a place within the group —one of the main desires of almost all students—and becomes a functioning part of the organism.

GROUP DYNAMICS

Previous paragraphs explained how roles and role expectations influence behavior. Membership in groups can affect individuals in other ways, too. Groups create their own psychological forces that strongly influence individuals. These forces are called group dynamics. Redl and Wattenberg describe some of the dynamics that cause difficulties in the classroom.

Contagious Behavior

Undesired behavior sometimes, but not always, spreads quickly in the classroom. One student's misbehavior may be a good sign of what other students are itching to do also. Once the ice is broken, other students may follow, especially if the perpetrator has high status.

Before reacting to misbehavior, teachers should evaluate its potential for spread. If the potential is high, teachers should squelch the misbehavior at once. If the potential is low, it may be safe to ignore the behavior or use a low-pressure technique such as suggesting the correct behavior.

Teachers can reduce contagion by giving attention to negative factors that foster it, including poor seating arrangements, boredom, restlessness, lack of purpose in lessons, and poor student manners. On the positive side, desirable behavior can also be contagious. Teachers can encourage positive behavior by approving it, reinforcing it, and giving status to those who display it.

Scapegoating

Scapegoating takes place when a group seeks to displace its hostility onto an unpopular individual or subgroup. The group will select a target person who is weak or outcast, often unable to cope with normal occurrences in the classroom. Scapegoating has undesirable consequences for everyone concerned. Teachers must guard against it and stifle it when it occurs. In so doing, they should be sure that their approach does not cause even more dislike for the target.

Teacher's Pets

When a group believes that a teacher is playing favorites, it reacts with jealousy and resentment. These emotions manifest themselves in hostile behavior toward the favored individual or group. Hostility may also be directed toward the teacher. When teachers need to give individual students extra help, they should be sure that the actions are seen as impartial, necessary, and professional.

Reactions To Strangers

It is common in most schools for strangers to enter the classroom occasionally. Teachers notice a marked change in student behavior when this occurs. Unknown visitors increase tension for teachers and students alike.

If the stranger is a new student, the group code may become exaggerated in order to show the newcomer how to act. For example, if the group prizes cooperation, they might go to great lengths to be helpful to the newcomer and each other. On the other hand, the group may set off a series of behaviors intended to test the new child. Individuals or subgroups may vie for friendship, offer status positions, or taunt each other.

If the stranger is an adult, the students may rally to support their teacher, if that person is liked and respected. If they do not respect their teacher they may misbehave rudely and boisterously. All teachers are well-advised to set up a standard procedure to be followed whenever a stranger enters the classroom.

Teachers should note the class reactions when a stranger enters the room. Extreme behaviors provide clues to underlying motivations and feelings that are operating within the group.

Group Disintegration

Groups serve many purposes, and good group behavior is highly desirable. Teachers hope to establish groups that will prosper, grow in maturity, and serve everyone well. Even the strongest group, however, will show strain in time.

Consider Mrs. Brown's discouraging situation. Early in the year her class worked strongly together, pulling toward goals as one. Later there was a decline in cohesion. One day when directing a lesson, Mrs. Brown noticed with dismay that some students were looking out the window, a small group was discussing the football game, and one student was writing a letter to a friend. The students had to be coerced into participating, one individual at a time.

Teachers frequently encounter such situations. Not knowing the cause, they are at a loss as to what to do or how to correct the situation. Redl and Wattenberg suggest that when a formerly effective group begins to disintegrate, teachers should ask themselves the following questions:

1. Are there long, unnecessary periods of waiting time where students could be getting more direction?
2. Are the assigned tasks relevant and within the students' ability?
3. Is there too much emphasis on competition between groups?
4. Are there too many unexpected changes in leadership, environment, schedules, and so forth?
5. Are the classroom activities stimulating and thought provoking?
6. Are students given ample opportunity to experience success, or are there too many failures?
7. Is there more criticism than praise from the teacher?

Each of these factors can cause problems within the group. As they appear, control problems appear with them. Group disintegration causes insecurity among members, especially weaker ones, in terms of knowing their place and their expected roles. This in turn causes deviant behavior and loss of mutual support within the group.

Comment on Group Dynamics

Group dynamics are psychological forces that influence individuals' behavior as members of a group. They are the forces behind the group's unwritten codes of conduct. When these codes run counter to teachers' codes, conflict occurs. Teachers are powerful, and they may seem to win out. However, the group code usually prevails under the surface, forming lasting attitudes that are the opposite of what the teacher desired.

PSYCHOLOGICAL ROLES OF TEACHERS

The ways in which groups and individuals behave in the classroom are greatly influenced by how they perceive the teacher. Like it or not,

16   EIGHT MODELS OF DISCIPLINE

teachers fill many different roles and present many different images. Some
of these roles and images are:

1. *Representatives of society.* Teachers reflect and develop values,
   moral attitudes, and thinking patterns typical of the community.
2. *Judges.* Teachers judge students' behavior, character, work, and
   progress.
3. *Source of knowledge.* Teachers are the primary source of knowledge, a resource from which to obtain information.
4. *Helpers in learning.* Teachers help students learn by giving directions, furnishing information, requiring that work be done, removing obstacles to learning, and facilitating problem solving.
5. *Referees.* Teachers arbitrate and make decisions when disputes
   arise.
6. *Detectives.* Teachers maintain security in the classroom, discover
   wrongdoing, and hand out consequences.
7. *Models.* Teachers model customs, manners, values, and beliefs
   that students are to imitate.
8. *Caretakers.* Teachers reduce anxiety by maintaining standards of
   behavior, consistent environments, regular schedules, and freedom from danger or threat.
9. *Ego supporters.* Teachers support student ego by building student
   self-confidence and bettering self-images.
10. *Group leaders.* Teachers facilitate harmonious and efficient group
    functioning.
11. *Surrogate parents.* Teachers are a source of protection, approval,
    affection, and advice.
12. *Targets for hostility.* When student hostility cannot be appropri-
    ately expressed to other adults, it may be displaced onto teachers.
13. *Friends and confidants.* Teachers can be talked with and confided
    in.
14. *Objects of affection.* Teachers are often objects of affection and
    esteem, as well as crushes and hero worship.

Comment On Psychological Roles Of Teachers. As you can see, teachers
are assigned many roles by students. Sometimes they have little choice
about those roles, but they can usually decide in part on the roles and on
how and when to assume them. They may assume some roles wholeheartedly and avoid others completely, depending on how they wish to relate to
students. Sometimes they may adopt or avoid certain roles, if they are
aware of a strong group need. In any event, teachers need to be sure that
they are steady and consistent in the roles they do assume.

DIAGNOSTIC THINKING IN THE CLASSROOM

So far we have examined several of Redl and Wattenberg's contentions—group makeup and functioning; group dynamics and how they affect class behavior; how group expectations can cause role-playing in individuals; and some of the many roles that students assign to teachers. Given this knowledge and an understanding of group motivation, how do teachers act on them?

Redl and Wattenberg suggest *diagnostic thinking* as a general approach to facing challenging situations. You will see that their approach is not a magical formula. It requires diligence and persistence. With practice, diagnostic thinking becomes second nature and allows teachers to add insights about psychological forces that influence group behavior and, in turn, permit efficient classroom management. Their diagnostic thinking approach involves *first hunch, fact gathering, hidden factors, acting,* and *flexibility.* They describe the approach as follows.

When conflict first becomes apparent, it is natural to form a *preliminary hunch* about its underlying cause. This hunch is not based on specific data, but is simply a general feeling about the incident.

Next, the teacher gathers *obvious facts.* Is there a student on the floor? Is he or she screaming and pointing at someone else? Is there something broken?

To these obvious facts the teacher adds *hidden factors* of which he or she may be aware. Hidden factors might be such things as background information on the students involved, knowledge of psychological, mental, or moral development, or knowledge of a previous volatile situation.

When teachers believe they have identified the facts, motivations, and other hidden factors behind a conflict, they are ready to *act* on the situation. This step is akin to testing a hypothesis; they apply a solution and see whether it works. The attempt may or may not solve the problem. After observing the effect of their actions, teachers may want to revise their appraisal or solution.

This uncertainty points out the need for teachers to be *flexible* in the diagnostic procedure. They may have assessed the situation incorrectly, or by their actions have altered its dynamics, thus creating a new situation that requires further action. Redl and Wattenberg suggest that a single action is not enough. Teachers must act in a series of steps, all leading ultimately to a resolution of the problem.

Redl and Wattenberg offer a final word of advice concerning diagnostic problem solving: Feelings are very important. Teachers should not rely solely on their own feelings, but should try to put themselves in the students' place, see how the students feel, and modify their actions accordingly.

See if you understand Mr. Bryant's use of diagnostic thinking in the following episode:

Three girls come into the classroom. Bonnie and Susan are in tears. Trish is shouting angrily. Class cannot proceed. There have been similar incidents during the last few weeks.

Mr. Bryant has a hunch that Trish is consistently instigating trouble between the other two. He examines the facts: Bonnie and Susan are usually upset; Trish is usually very vocal; these problems occur at the end of the week. From their exchanges Mr. Bryant deduces a hidden factor—Trish wants Bonnie to go to the football game with her, not with Susan.

Mr. Bryant now must decide on a course of action, knowing that it may or may not work. He asks himself, "Should I give some sort of situational assistance? Would reality appraisal work? Is punishment called for in this case?" He is trying to decide on "influence techniques." Look for descriptions of what he has in mind in the next section.

INFLUENCE TECHNIQUES

Redl and Wattenberg have given much attention to the kinds of acts that teachers use to resolve problem behavior. Acts are only a part of diagnostic thinking, but are the obvious manifestations of the process. Redl and Wattenberg called these acts "influence techniques."

Every teacher uses several different techniques to maintain classroom control. Some of those techniques are based on school disciplinary policies; some are selected because they reflect teachers' personalities and philosophies; and others are used because teachers have found them to work well in the past. Some are very effective and some are not effective at all. Many are applicable in certain situations but not in others.

Situations arise regularly that call for corrective action. Teachers use a variety of means for making those corrections. Some shout, some remove students from the class, some suggest alternative behaviors, some ignore the misbehavior. Redl and Wattenberg urge teachers to learn to ask themselves a series of rapid-fire questions before they take action:

1. What is the motivation behind the misbehavior?
2. How is the classs reacting?
3. Is the misbehavior related to interaction with the teacher?
4. How will the student react when corrected?
5. How will the correction affect future behavior?

Answers to these questions help ensure first that teachers understand the situation, and then that they will be able to choose a corrective technique that has positive influence on the misbehaving student. Redl and Wattenberg describe four categories of influence techniques from which teachers can choose in accord with the answers to the questions above. The categories are: (1) supporting self-control, (2) offering situational assistance, (3) appraising reality, and (4) invoking the pain-pleasure principle. It must be remembered that if any of these techniques are to be most effective, students must know exactly what the issues are and how they are expected to behave. Expectations and consequences should be made clear at the beginning of the class.

Supporting Self-Control

Most students, most of the time, want to behave correctly and gain the teacher's approval. They do not misbehave simply because they want to be unpleasant. When misbehavior occurs, it is due to some other reason (that is why teachers should appraise the situation). Often it is nothing more than a lapse in self-control, and in that case the best corrective technique is to help students regain control of their own behavior.

Techniques for supporting self-control are low keyed. They are not forceful, aggressive, or punitive, but aim at helping students help themselves. Teachers should use them when they feel that students are on the verge of losing control. In this way behavior is checked before it becomes unacceptable.

Redl and Wattenberg describe five techniques for supporting self-control. The first technique is *sending signals*. With this technique teachers use signs that show they know what is going on and that they don't approve. Examples are making eye contact, frowning, shaking the head. These signals are most effective during the earliest stages of misbehavior.

If students fail to respond to a signal, teachers may want to try *proximity control*. By moving closer to the offender, teachers communicate that they are aware and want to help. This allows the student to draw strength from the nearness of the teacher and use that strength to regain self-control. It is usually enough simply to move closer to the student, but sometimes a friendly touch on the shoulder or head might be needed.

Sometimes students who have good self-control will begin to misbehave when they lose interest in an assignment. Teachers can correct this by going to students and *showing interest* in their work. A teacher might say to one, "I see you've finished the first five problems. I'll bet you'll finish them all before the end of the period." This technique is not effective, of course, if the student is lost or feels unable to do the assignment.

A pleasant way to make students aware of a lapse in control is with *humor*. It is important that this humor be gentle and always accompanied by a smile from the teacher. An example of humor would be, "My, there is so much chattering, I almost forgot for a minute that I was in a classroom." Teachers must be careful that they do not use sarcasm or ridicule in such statements. Those are punishing techniques, not supporting techniques.

Occasionally, *ignoring* is one of the most appropriate support techniques, especially if a student is testing a situation. When the teacher ignores inappropriate behavior it often clues other students in the class to follow suit, thus discouraging behavior used to gain attention. However, teachers should be cautious in using this technique because students might interpret it as insecurity or indecisiveness.

Comment On Supportive Techniques. Techniques that support self-control are useful, but they also have disadvantages. When used in the early stages of misbehavior, they can eliminate the need to dole out penalties, and they give students much needed opportunities to work on controlling their own behavior. It should be remembered, however, that these techniques are effective only in situations where misbehavior is mild or just beginning. If supportive techniques don't get the message across, firmer, more direct techniques are required.

Providing Situational Assistance

When misbehavior reaches the point that students cannot regain self-control, teachers must step in with assistance to guide students back onto the proper course. Redl and Wattenberg describe several techniques for providing situational assistance.

Hurdle help is one such technique. Suppose a math assignment has been made. Susan begins working only to discover she has no understanding of the procedure required. She begins to talk to another student. In this case, the teacher needs only to help Susan over the hurdle, not attack her because she is talking and not working.

Another technique in providing situational assistance is *restructuring or rescheduling the situation*. Mr. James's students have come in to class after participating in a particularly exciting volleyball match. He knows that it will be difficult for the students to get to work in his math class. Instead of the routine math assignment, he decides to use the game's scores to solve some computation problems. Why did he change his plans?

When behavior problems are caused by restlessness or overexcitement teachers should recognize the cause—perhaps students have been made to sit too long, or have had too many exciting activities in too short a time. Teachers can restructure situations by giving a brief period of rest, changing the nature of the activities, or rescheduling the work for a more appropriate time.

On the other hand, a lack of established routines can also cause problems because students do not know exactly what they should be doing, or when. Teachers assist in this situation by *establishing routines* and thus adding consistency and predictability to the curriculum. Routines are especially helpful in activities that are apt to become complex or confusing, or where there are many students involved.

If one student has temporarily lost self-control and is disturbing the rest of the class, the teacher might decide to *remove the student from the situation*. Travis refuses to take his seat for a lesson. The teacher takes his hand and leads him to the far corner of the room telling him, "When you decide to sit down, you may return to join us."

This should always be done in a nonpunitive way. The teacher should emphasize that the student is only exiled until self-control is regained. When a student must be removed from the group, it is important to follow up later with a private talk. Feelings of both teacher and student should be discussed.

Attractive objects that students have in their possession—photographs, toys, etc.—can sometimes overpower self-control. In such cases teachers need only *remove the seductive object*. This is a temporary measure and should be explained to the student as such, together with provisions for returning the object to the student.

Sometimes a lapse in self-control may cause a student to become a danger to her or himself and others. When this happens, the teacher may have to use *physical restraint*. When restraint is used as a situational assistance technique, great care must be taken not to hurt the student. Restraint should be neither rough nor punitive, but should be merely containing or restraining until control is regained.

Comment On Providing Situational Assistance. Many different situations can cause students to lose self-control temporarily. In such cases, punitive measures are not needed; in fact, punishment is counterproductive. Instead, the teacher provides only the assistance needed to help students regain control. This approach has many advantages, such as reducing confusion, allowing students to keep energy and attention focused on learning, and establishing the teacher's posture as one of helpfulness and kindliness.

Reality Appraisal

Student misbehavior often escalates for reasons that are not evident even to the students who are misbehaving. Behavior can be improved markedly when teachers help students to examine a behavior situation, see the underlying causes, and foresee the probable consequences. This is what Redl and Wattenberg refer to as reality appraisal, and they have suggested a variety of things teachers should keep in mind when using this approach.

Too often teachers overlook the simplest method for dealing with students, which is to *tell it like it is*. Teachers do this by explaining exactly why behavior is inappropriate and outlining clear connections between conduct and consequences. Teachers should not underestimate students' ability to comprehend statements such as: "If everyone talks at once, no one gets heard;" or "Pushing and horsing around can cause injuries;" or "If you don't keep up with assignments, you simply won't learn very much." Students usually respond well to rules whose reasons they understand, and they judge teachers who take time to explain the rules to be just and fair.

Obviously, one key to reality appraisal is *clarity*. Teachers must make it very clear to students which behaviors are inappropriate, why they are inappropriate, what the probable consequences will be, and what students should do instead.

When using reality appraisal, teachers often must give criticism. Since few people respond positively to criticism, teachers must strive to express it in ways that *show encouragement*. Criticism should be offered in ways that stimulate efforts to try harder; it should not frustrate students with impossible expectations. Neither should it attack students' personal values, humiliate them, or otherwise hurt their self-image or prestige. The teacher's role is to support, not to attack or blame.

Students often misbehave for no other reason than to test limits. They need the security of knowing exactly how far they will be able to go. *Setting limits* provides this security by telling students clearly what is expected, what is unacceptable, and why. Teachers should remember that setting limits and enforcing rules are separate issues. Making threats while setting limits indicates that the teacher expects violations.

Comments On Reality Appraisal. Appraising the reality of a situation helps students to see underlying aspects of situations, themselves, and others, thereby assisting them in developing their own values. This enables them to act more appropriately in future situations.

At times, especially during disturbing incidents, emotions run strong, and both teacher and students are apt to make inappropriate comments. It is difficult for both parties to listen to what is being said. For that reason, Redl and Wattenberg believe discussions about the incident should be held sometime afterward, when both parties are calmer and better able to talk over what happened. This talk is not a time for lecturing or scolding, but rather a time to sort out causes and feelings. It is important for teachers to understand why students acted as they did, and equally important for students to understand the teacher's actions. Such discussions may make it easier to handle similar situations in the future.

Invoking the Pain-Pleasure Principle

When behavior problems persist despite the teacher's attempts to support student self-control, provide situational assistance, and appraise reality, it becomes necessary to move to the strongest measure in Redl and Wattenberg's suggestions—invoking the pain-pleasure principle. The meaning of this approach is evident, but becomes clearer through the understanding that they are really referring to a "pain principle," with little to say about the effects of pleasure.

Pain, for Redl and Wattenberg, is not harsh punishment, but rather consequences that are unpleasant to the student. They do use the word punishment; therefore it is important to recognize the benign nature of the unpleasant consequences they suggest. In contrast, pleasure refers to consequences that are pleasant to the student. Let us examine these meanings a bit further:

Punishment. When students lose the battle for self-control, it sometimes becomes necessary to resort to punishment. Punishment should consist of planned, unpleasant consequences, the purpose of which is to modify behavior in positive directions. Punishment should not be physical, nor should it involve angry outbursts that indicate lack of self-control on the part of the teacher. Neither should it be actions taken to get back at misbehaving students, or to "teach them a lesson." Instead, it should require them to make amends for breaking rules, do correctly what was done incorrectly, forego activities they enjoy, and so forth.

Even when punishing, teachers should try to communicate the idea that they like the students and are trying to help them. Students should be made to see punishment as a *natural and understandable consequence* of unacceptable behavior. If students sense good intentions from the teacher, they will be at least partly angry at themselves for losing self-control, not at the teacher who is trying to help them regain it.

Punishment should be used only as a last resort, when other approaches have failed. That is because there are many things that can go · wrong when punishment is used, such as:

1. Punishment is used as revenge or release from tension.
2. It has detrimental effects on student self-concept and relations with the teacher.
3. Over time it reduces student ability to maintain self-control.

4. Students may use it to raise status with peers.
5. It presents an undesirable model for solving problems.

Threats and Promises

The pain principle should be seen by students and teachers as a *promise*, an assurance that unpleasant consequences will follow repeated inappropriate behavior. Promises can be made without negative emotion, and they do not promote undue fear or other negative reactions in students.

Threats, on the other hand, make students anxious and fearful, which may interfere with learning and certainly work to the detriment of a positive classroom climate. Threats tend to be harsh and negative, taking the form of "If you don't...I will...." Teachers who make dire threats seldom carry them out, and that is often their undoing; their ability to control misbehavior erodes, as does their ability to relate positively with the class.

Instead of making threats, teachers should simply state which behaviors are unacceptable and explain exactly what the consequences will be for those behaviors. Unlike threats, these calm assertions lend security to the classroom and help students maintain their own self-control.

FRITZ REDL'S SUGGESTIONS

Essentialy, Redl and Wattenberg's suggestions are based on common sense applications of humane personal relations. Their overall view is summarized nicely by Fritz Redl in his book *When We Deal With Children* (1966):

1. Give students a say in setting standards and deciding consequences. Let them tell how they think you should handle situations that call for punishment.
2. Keep students' emotional health in mind at all times. Punished students must feel that the teacher likes them. *Always* talk to students about their feelings after the situation has calmed down.
3. Be helpful, not hurtful. Show students you want to support their best behaviors.
4. Punishment does not work well. Use it as a last resort. Try other approaches first.
5. Don't be afraid to change your course of action if you get new insights into a situation.
6. Remember: mistakes in discipline need not be considered disastrous, unless they are repeated.

7. Be objective, maintain humor, and remember that we are all human.

Application Exercises

NOTE: For each of the eight models, the same two cases—nonworking Kris and hostile Tom—will be used to illustrate and practice each authority's advice on dealing with misbehavior.

CASE #1. KRIS WILL NOT WORK:

There is a common behavior that frustrates teachers at all levels. It is one in which students do not participate in classroom activities. The students are neither disruptive nor hostile; the problem is simply that it is very difficult to get them to complete their assignments or even join in the classroom happenings. They just sit there like bumps on a log.

  Kris, in Mr. Jake's class, behaves in that manner. She is quite docile. She never disrupts class and does little socializing with other students. She rarely completes an assignment. She is simply there, putting forth almost no effort.

How would Redl and Wattenberg deal with Kris? Redl and Wattenberg would suggest that teachers take the following steps in attempting to improve Kris's classroom behavior.

1. Follow the steps in diagnostic thinking: develop a hunch; gather facts; try to discover hidden factors; apply a solution; try out another solution if the first does not work. That might lead to questions such as: Does Kris have emotional problems? Are things difficult for her at home? Is she withdrawing into a fantasy life? Will a warm caring approach help?
2. Depending on the conclusions reached in diagnostic thinking, the teacher would try out one or more of the following solutions:
   a) Sending signals to Kris (I know you are not working).
   b) Moving closer to prompt Kris into action.
   c) Showing a special interest in Kris's work.
   d) Employing humor (I know you'll want to finish this in my lifetime!).
   e) Offering assistance to Kris.
   f) Telling it like it is (Each incomplete assignment causes you to fall further behind and affects your grade!).
   g) Removing Kris from the situation (You can return when you have completed your work).

CASE #2. TOM IS HOSTILE AND DEFIANT:

Tom has appeared to be in his usual foul mood ever since arriving in class. He gets up and on his way to sharpen his pencil he bumps into Frank. Frank complains. Tom tells him loudly to shut up. Miss Baines, the teacher, says "Tom, go back to your seat." Tom wheels around, swears loudly and says heatedly "I'll go when I'm damned good and ready!"

How would Redl and Wattenberg have Miss Baines deal with Tom?

QUESTIONS:

1. Were Kris and Tom playing any of the roles identified by Redl and Wattenberg?
2. What psychological roles might Kris and Tom expect their teachers to fill?
3. What roles are the following students playing?
   a) Cheryl strolls into Spanish class five minutes late. "Que pasa?" she says nonchalantly to the teacher. The class laughs.
   b) The auto shop teacher notices a group of boys squirting oil at one another. The boys point to Shaun who is watching from the sidelines. "He started it," they all agree. Although untrue, Shaun grins and does not deny it.
4. How would Redl and Wattenberg suggest that the respective teachers deal with the Cheryl and Shaun situations?

REFERENCES

Redl, F. (1972). *When we deal with children: selected writings*. New York: Free Press.

Redl, F., & Wattenberg, W. (1951; 1959). *Mental hygiene in teaching*. New York: Harcourt, Brace and World.

Sheviakov, G., & Redl, F. (1956). *Discipline for today's children*. Washington, D.C.: Association for Supervision and Curriculum Development.

Wattenberg, W. (1955). *The adolescent years*. New York: Harcourt Brace.

Wattenberg, W. (1967). *All men are created equal*. Detroit: Wayne State University Press.

CHAPTER 2

The Kounin Model:
Withitness, Alerting, and Group Management

KOUNIN BIOGRAPHICAL SKETCH

Jacob Kounin was born in Cleveland, Ohio, on January 17, 1912. He received his doctorate in 1939 from Iowa State University. In 1946 he was appointed to a professorship at Wayne State University, where he has since served as a professor of educational psychology. Dr. Kounin has made numerous presentations to the American Psychological Association, the American Educational Research Association, and many other organizations. He has served often as a consultant and visiting professor at other universities.

Dr. Kounin is best known for his work *Discipline and Group Management in Classrooms* (1971; 1977), a book that grew out of two decades of research. In the earlier years, his studies focused on group management, with emphasis on how handling the misbehavior of one student affected other students. Kounin observed that a general effect occurred in the group, which he called the *ripple effect*.

From ripple effect studies came subsequent research on disciplinary and group management techniques. This research involved videotapes made in 80 different classrooms. Kounin analyzed the thousands of hours of tape and discovered several dimensions of group management that promoted student involvement and reduced the amount of misbehavior.

KOUNIN'S CENTRAL FOCUS

Good classroom behavior depends on effective lesson management, especially on pacing, transitions, alerting, and individual accountability.

Kounin's Key Ideas

1. When teachers correct misbehavior in one student, it often influences the behavior of nearby students. This is known as the ripple effect.
2. Teachers should know what is going on in all parts of the classroom at all times. Kounin called this awareness, "withitness."
3. The ability to provide smooth transitions between activities and to maintain consistent momentum within activities is crucial to effective group management.
4. Teachers should strive to maintain group alertness and to hold every group member accountable for the content of a lesson, which allows optimal learning to occur.
5. Student satiation (boredom) can be avoided by providing a feeling

of progress and by adding variety to curriculum and classroom environment.

THE RIPPLE EFFECT

Kounin's research on the ripple effect started accidentally one day when he reprimanded a college student for reading a newspaper during the lecture. Immediately afterward, he noticed a difference in the behavior of other students in the class. They sat up straighter and paid closer attention. Kounin's observation led him to believe that the way in which teachers issue desists (remarks intended to stop misbehavior) also influences the behavior of students who merely witness the desist. The effect of the desist ripples from the target student outward to others.

Kounin then tested the ripple effect in four different settings—college, kindergarten, high school, and summer camp. In the college study he set up an experiment to compare the effects of a "supporting desist" (offering to help) versus a "threatening desist" (chastising the student). Both produced a ripple effect.

In the kindergarten study, Kounin tried to determine whether the *quality* of a desist influenced the degree of conforming behavior. The three qualities tested were (1) *clarity*, with information that named the deviant, specified the unacceptable behavior, and gave reasons for the desist; (2) *firmness*, that is, projecting an "I mean it" attitude until the misbehavior stopped; and (3) *roughness*, in which the desist included anger, physical handling, and punishment. Kounin found that:

1. Clarity increased conforming behavior of students who witnessed the desist.
2. Firmness increased conformity only in students who were misbehaving at the time.
3. Roughness did not improve behavior at all; it simply upset the audience children, making them restless and anxious.

Kounin also found that the ripple effect was very pronounced on the first day of school but tended to diminish as the year wore on.

In the summer camp study, Kounin attempted to measure the ripple effect with children from 7 to 13 years of age. He could find no measurable effect and decided that this was due to the fact that misconduct at camp was considered more acceptable than at home or school and resulted in fewer consequences. Children in summer camp did not take desists seriously.

In the high school study, Kounin found that the type of desist had no effect on the amount of misbehavior exhibited by the audience students.

He found that an extremely angry outburst by the teacher caused some emotional discomfort in students witnessing the desist. What did influence behavior in high school students was the degree to which the teacher was liked. High regard for the teacher coupled with high motivation to learn created maximum work involvement and minimum misbehavior among students.

From these studies one can conclude the following: The ripple effect may occur as the teacher gives encouragement ("Good, I see that many of you are almost finished") and as the teacher gives reprimands ("I see a few people who may have to stay in after class to finish"). The ripple effect is most powerful at the elementary level. It is weaker at the secondary and college levels where it depends on the popularity or prestige of the teacher.

WITHITNESS

Kounin coined the term "withitness" to describe teachers' knowing what was going on in all areas of the classroom at all times. It is akin to the familiar "eyes in the back of the head." Kounin determined that this trait is communicated more effectively by teachers' behaviors than by their words, and further, that it is effective only if students are convinced that the teacher really knows what is going on. If Bob and Bill are not working, the teacher's behavior or words must clearly communicate, "I see you have not started. This must be done today!"

Kounin found two elements of withitness that contributed to effectiveness. The first is the ability to select the correct student for a desist. Suppose Bob and Bill are teasing Mary while the teacher is at work elsewhere with a small group. Mary finally says in a loud voice, "Stop that you two!" The teacher tells Mary to go sit alone, giving no attention to the instigators of the incident. This tells the students that the teacher does not know what is really going on.

The second element is attending to the more serious deviancy when two are occurring simultaneously. To illustrate: Jill is playing with a toy at her desk. Meanwhile, James and Eric are pushing each other violently at the drinking fountain. The teacher looks up and says, "Jill, bring that toy up to me and get back to work." The teacher failed to take any action against the fight at the drinking fountain. If mistakes like this occur often, students begin to realize that the teacher is not truly aware. This encourages them to misbehave without fear of being caught.

Timing also influences withitness. A major mistake in timing is to wait until the misbehavior spreads before taking action. A student throws a paper ball at the wastebasket. Another student sees this and decides to try it. Three or four others join into the shooting contest. This does not occur when teachers correct the misbehavior as it first occurs. Proper timing shows students that the teacher knows exactly what is going on.

Another timing mistake is to allow the misbehavior to increase in seriousness before stopping it. Let's return to the example of the two boys at the drinking fountain. James went there to get a drink. Eric pushed his way in front of James. James pushed him out of the way claiming he was there first. Eric hit James, James hit back, and they began to scuffle. The teacher had waited too long to intervene. If she had been aware of what was happening, she could have spoken to the boys early and stopped the misbehavior.

Kounin found that if students perceive that teachers are with it (in that they choose the right culprit and correct misbehavior at once), they are less likely to misbehave, especially in teacher-directed lessons. Handling the correct deviant on time is more important to classroom control than is firmness or clarity of a desist.

OVERLAPPING

In his videotape studies, Kounin became aware of a group-management technique that he labeled *overlapping*. Overlapping is the ability to attend to two issues at the same time. Here is an example. A teacher is meeting with a small group and notices that two students at their seats are playing cards instead of doing their assignment. The teacher could correct this either by:

1. Stopping the small group activity, walking over to the card players and getting them back on task, and then attempting to reestablish the small-group work; or
2. Having the small group continue while addressing the card players from a distance, then monitoring the students at their desks while conducting the small-group activity.

As you can tell, the second approach involves overlapping. Teachers are often interrupted while working with groups or individuals. A student may approach with a paper that must be reviewed before the student can continue. Teachers adroit in overlapping can check the paper while glancing at the small group and adding encouraging remarks such as "Go on," or "That's correct." Thus, the teacher attends to two issues simultaneously.

Not surprisingly Kounin found that teachers who were adept at overlapping were also aware of the broader scope of happenings in the classroom. They were more with it. Overlapping loses its effectiveness if the teacher does not also demonstrate withitness. If students working independently know that the teacher is aware of them and able to deal with them, they are more likely to remain on task.

MOVEMENT MANAGEMENT

Kounin's research revealed an important relationship between student behavior and *movement* within and between lessons. He did not mean physical movement of students or teachers. He meant lesson movement—*pacing, momentum, and transitions*. Teachers' ability to move smoothly from one activity to the next and to maintain momentum within an activity has a great deal to do with their effectiveness in controlling behavior in the classroom. In smooth transitions, student attention is turned easily from one activity to another, thus keeping student attention on the task at hand.

Kounin discovered two transition mistakes—jerkiness and slow-downs—that seem to encourage student misbehavior. *Jerkiness* describes the failure to move smoothly from one activity to another. Suppose high school students are working on an art project. Unexpectedly, the teacher says "Put your supplies away and get ready for a visitor." Half the class does not hear and the other half starts to move around in confusion. Or suppose an elementary class has just begun a math lesson. The teacher calls on three students to go the the board. On their way up she suddenly asks, "How many of you brought your money for the field trip?" She then counts the raised hands, goes to her desk, and writes down the number.

Kounin gives many other examples of jerkiness in moving from one activity to another. They cause confusion, unnecessary activity, noise, delay, and misbehavior. These problems are minimized with smooth transitions, resulting from routines, clear directions, and completing one task before beginning another.

A second transition mistake Kounin discovered was one he called *slowdowns*. These are delays that waste time between activities. A typical slowdown comes from what Kounin called overdwelling, that is, spending too much time giving directions and explanations or lecturing students about inappropriate behavior. Another type of slowdown occurs when teachers spend too much time on the details, rather than the main idea of a lesson. Suppose Mr. Anderson is doing a math lesson with the class. He writes some problems on the board for students to complete. He stops them frequently to insert comments such as "Make sure you leave space at the margins," "Remember to skip lines between problems," "Don't forget to number each problem," "Don't put more than three problems on a line," "Be sure to put boxes around your answers." These comments break student concentration and slow their progress.

Transitions may seem at first to be minor concerns, but Kounin concluded from his investigations that *teachers' ability to manage smooth transitions and maintain momentum was more important to work involvement and classroom control than any other behavior-management technique.*

GROUP FOCUS

Teachers have few opportunities to work exclusively with one student. Mostly they work with groups, sometimes the entire class, and sometimes several smaller groups concurrently. Kounin found that the ability to maintain a concerted group focus—that is, keeping students paying attention to the same thing at the same time—is essential to a productive, efficient classroom. Teachers are better able to maintain group focus when they take into account the (1) *group format*, (2) *degree of accountability* of each student for the content of the lesson, and (3) effective focus of group *attention*.

Group Format

Group format refers to grouping students in such a manner that maximum active participation is encouraged. Generally speaking this is obtained through larger, rather than smaller groups. Larger groups allow teachers to call on many different students instead of a few. When responses are desired, the teacher may ask the group to respond in unison, or one student may be asked to do an activity at the chalkboard while the remaining members of the group follow by doing the activity at their seats. Having everyone involved in an activity eliminates the group waiting for one member to perform.

Accountability

Accountability refers to each student in the group being responsible for learning each of the facts, concepts, or procedures being taught in a lesson. It is enhanced when teachers know exactly how each student is progressing. Kounin recommends several techniques for holding all members of a group accountable:

1. All students hold up response props for the teacher to see.
2. The teacher asks all members to observe and check on accuracy while one group member performs.

3. The teacher asks all members to write the answer and then at random calls on various students to respond.
4. The teacher circulates and observes the responses of nonreciters.
5. The teacher calls for a unison response and then checks individuals at random.

Group accountability has much in common with overlapping. The teacher is able to deal with the entire group and yet have individuals show accountability for their progress. When students perceive that the teacher will definitely and immediately hold them accountable for the content of the lesson, they are more likely to pay attention and remain involved in the activity.

Attention

Attention is a third element in group focus. Group alerting involves focusing the attention of all group members on the activity at all times. Kounin advocates the following for maintaining attentive group focus:

1. The teacher attracts attention by looking around the group in a suspenseful manner, or saying "Let's see who can..."
2. The teacher keeps in suspense who will be called on next and avoids a predictable pattern of response.
3. The teacher varies unison responses with individual responses.
4. Nonreciters are alerted that they may be called on in connection with a reciter's response: "Listen to Jim as he reads and see if you can guess who took the crystal ball."

All of these practices draw the attention of the group to the lesson, alerting every member.

Kounin also examined some common mistakes that contribute to non-attention within the group:

1. The teacher focuses on one student at a time and excludes the other members from the lesson.
2. The teacher chooses a reciter before asking a question, allowing others to stop listening because they know they won't have to respond.
3. The teacher calls on students to respond in a predictable sequence, such as going clockwise around a circle. Students then only need to be ready to respond after their neighbor. This permits them to allow their attention to wander. (It is interesting to note that recent research casts some doubt on points 2 and 3. Some studies have

shown slightly higher achievement in classes where students are called on in a predictable sequence.)

Of the three elements of group focus, Kounin found maintaining attention to be the most important. Teachers who held the attention of every member throughout the lesson were more successful at inducing work involvement and preventing misbehavior. As one might suspect, group accountability and attention accompany each other, and both come into play to a greater extent in teacher-directed lessons than in lessons where students work independently.

AVOIDING SATIATION

Satiation means getting filled up with something, getting enough of it, getting bored. Kounin used the term to describe a change in the dynamics of an activity where students show progressively less interest. Other behaviors may begin to surface, as well. For instance, students may introduce spontaneous variations into the activity. If made to write multiplication facts 10 times each they may after a time start writing the top line of the problem across the paper, then adding the multiplication sign, then adding the bottom digits, and so so, rather than completing each problem separately.

Satiation causes careless work that results in increased errors. Students begin to do the work mechanically, devoting little thought to the process. The result is a breakdown in meaning. When students break up an activity in a different way to add variety, they may also lose their grasp of the process or concept being learned.

Satiated students not only tend to become less involved in an activity, they may try to escape from it. This is often shown in behaviors such as looking out the window, tying shoes, poking a neighbor, or needlessly sharpening a pencil. They look for anything to initiate some new type of stimulation.

Since satiation may interfere seriously with learning and good behavior, teachers are admonished to prevent its occurrence. As remedies, Kounin suggests providing progress, challenge, and variety.

Progress

Kounin studied many different classrooms to determine why some teachers induced more satiation than did others. One element that more effective teachers used to reduce satiation was providing the students a feeling of progress. Students who saw they were making definite progress took longer to become satiated. Those who did the same task over and over, without feeling they were progressing, satiated quickly.

Challenge

Kounin also noticed that teachers who offered challenges throughout a lesson forestalled satiation. One of the many ways they provided challenges was to show enthusiasm for the lesson with remarks like "I have a special magical math formula to teach you today." Another way was to elicit positive feelings about the lesson by saying something like "I know you'll all get the answer to the next one!" Teachers might make comments such as "Don't be fooled by this one. It's tricky!" These techniques work if the teacher is genuinely enthusiastic and positive.

Variety

Variety is not only the spice of life; it is the spice of most lessons. Kounin felt that variety plays a crucial role in reducing satiation and suggested that teachers vary their classroom activities. Elementary teachers, for example, might have a quiet reading time, followed by physical education, followed by math, and then a spelling game. Secondary teachers might alternate reading, discussion activities, creative production, and independent inquiry.

Within lessons teachers may change the level of intellectual challenge. Sometimes students may simply listen. At other times they may practice a skill or demonstrate comprehension of concepts. The teacher may challenge them by having them engage in abstract thinking or exhibit some sort of creativity.

Teachers can also vary the way they present lessons. They can demonstrate, direct an activity, ask questions for discussion, or have students solve problems on their own. While monitoring the students they may circulate among them or participate in the activities. Students enjoy variety in styles or presentation as well as variety among lessons, even when covering the same material.

Variety can also be provided in the materials used to enhance or extend learning. Some activities call for the usual pencil and paper, but others can make excellent use of slides, tape recorders, or such unusual things as live snakes or real musicians.

Finally, restructuring groups can add variety. One may start a lesson with the entire class, break into small groups for close interaction, and then reconvene into the whole class. The focus changes from teacher to students and back to teacher. Variety is provided through movement and different kinds of interacting and thinking.

COMMENTS ON KOUNIN'S MODEL

The techniques advocated by Kounin for class control are all intended to create and maintain a classroom atmosphere conducive to learning. By keeping students busily (and happily) engaged, behavior problems are reduced to a minimum.

In order to function as Kounin suggests, teachers must be able to deal with the entire class, various subgroups, and individual students, often at the same time. Kounin does not believe that teachers' personality traits are particularly important in classroom control. What is important, he insists, is teachers' ability to manage groups and lessons. To reiterate, teachers must learn to:

1. Know what is happening in every area of the classroom at all times and communicate that fact to students.
2. Be able to deal with more than one issue at a time.
3. Correct the appropriate target before misbehavior escalates.
4. Ensure smooth transitions from one activity to another.
5. Maintain group focus through alerting and accountability.
6. Provide nonsatiating learning programs by emphasizing progress, challenge, and variety.

Kounin's ideas have been widely acknowledged and received. Most of today's discipline systems incorporate his findings, as will become evident as the remaining models are presented. There is no doubt of the value of his suggestions in maintaining a good learning environment, one that also prevents misbehavior. For that reason his suggestions fit best into the *preventive* facet of discipline. As an entire system of discipline, however, teachers find that Kounin's suggestions are of less help in supportive discipline and almost no help at all in the techniques of *corrective* discipline, where misbehavior must be stopped and redirected positively.

Application Exercises

NOTE: Again, Kris and Tom will be used for the exercise.

CASE #1. KRIS WILL NOT WORK:

Kris, in Mr. Jake's class, is quite docile. She never disrupts class and does little socializing with other students. But despite Mr. Jake's best efforts, Kris rarely completes an assignment. She doesn't seem to care. She is simply there, putting forth virtually no effort.

How would Kounin deal with Kris? Kounin would suggest to teachers that they use the following sequence of interventions until they find one that is effective with Kris.

1. Use the ripple effect. "I see many people have already completed half their work." Look at Kris. Later comment, "I'm afraid a few people will have to stay late to complete their work."
2. Let Kris know you are aware she is not working. Say to her, "I see you have barely started. This work must be done today!"
3. Call on Kris in discussions preceeding independent work, as a means of involving her in the lesson.
4. Point out Kris's progress when it occurs: "Good! Now you are on the track! Keep up the good work."
5. Provide variety. Continually challenge Kris to accomplish more.
6. Hold Kris accountable with group focus techniques. Do not disregard her just because she has been nonproductive.

CASE #2. TOM IS HOSTILE AND DEFIANT:

Tom has appeared to be in his usual foul mood ever since arriving in class. He gets up and on his way to sharpen his pencil he bumps into Frank. Frank complains. Tom tells him loudly to shut up. Miss Baines, the teacher, says "Tom, go back to your seat." Tom wheels around, swears loudly and says heatedly "I'll go when I'm damned good and ready!"

What advice has Kounin provided to help Miss Baines deal with Tom?

QUESTIONS:

1. How do you think withitness and the ripple effect would work with Kris? With Tom?
2. How might Kris's behavior affect others in the class? How could the bad effects, if any, be reduced?
3. How might Tom's behavior affect others in the class? How could the bad effects, if any, be reduced?
4. According to Kounin's findings, (a) which students in the class would be most affected by the following teacher actions and comments, and (b) how would they be affected?
   Mr. Kent says, "Kevin, I see you bothering Brian while you are supposed to be working. In this class we keep our hands to ourselves."
   Mr. Kent says, "Kevin, stop that immediately! I will not allow that in my classroom!"
   Mr. Kent grabs Kevin by the arm and sits him in a chair, shouting, "You stop that!"
5. Evaluate the following to determine where, and to what extent, satiation might become a problem. Explain your conclusions.
   Mr. Kent does not allow students to move ahead into a new unit of work until all students have completed the old unit with passing scores. Those who pass early are given review and practice pages until the others catch up.

Mr. Grant allows students to move on to the next unit as soon as they can get a passing score. He helps slower students who need more work to learn the concepts.

During his 50-minute period Mr. Smith usually provides some direct instruction, some small-group activity, and some independent work.

6. One of the things Ms. Alletto's students like best about her is that she never pressures them to move quickly from one activity to the next. She seems to understand their need to talk with each other about nonschool matters. She always waits until all the class gets ready before she begins a new lesson or activity. What would Kounin say about Ms. Alletto's tolerant approach?

REFERENCES

Kounin, J. (1971; 1977). *Discipline and group management in classrooms.* New York: Holt, Rinehart and Winston.

CHAPTER 3

The Neo-Skinnerian Model:
Shaping Desired Behavior

SKINNER BIOGRAPHICAL SKETCH

B. F. Skinner, considered by many to be the greatest behavioral psychologist of all time, was born in Susquehanna, Pennsylvania, on March 20, 1904. He earned his PhD in psychology at Harvard in 1931 and has spent most of his subsequent career at that University. There he conducted his famous experimental studies in learning.

Earlier behaviorism had been concerned with stimulus-response connections. Skinner looked at the learning process in the opposite way, investigating how learning was affected by stimuli presented *after* an act was performed. He found that certain stimuli caused the organism to repeat an act more frequently. He called stimuli with that effect *reinforcers*. He found that by providing reinforcers in a systematic way (called reinforcement) one could shape behavior in desired directions.

Skinner's work was not confined to laboratory animals. He drew world-wide attention for his ideas about raising infants inside glass enclosures called air cribs where the child was kept dry, warm, and comfortable, with all needs satisfied. He raised his own daughter in an air crib.

Skinner drew much attention, too, with the publication of his novel *Walden Two* (1948), which described the workings of a utopian community that made extensive use of the principles of reinforcement. It is still widely read and has served as a model for communes in various places.

In 1971 Skinner's book *Beyond Freedom and Dignity* was published, and again world attention turned to him. He challenged traditional concepts of freedom and dignity as inadequate, insisting they are outmoded, useless, and incorrect. We are not free to choose, he asserted. Our choices are made, instead, on the basis of what has happened to us in the past; that is, on the reinforcements we have received for prior actions. Instead of concentrating on free choice, we should turn our efforts to providing conditions that improve human behavior in general.

Teachers have benefited most from Skinner's fundamental work in reinforcement as a means of controlling and motivating student behavior. Skinner's work has been enlarged, extended, and modified by numerous psychologists and educators. Its various applications to classroom practice are commonly called *behavior modification*, a technique that many teachers consider to be one of their most valuable tools for improving both learning and behavior of their students.

SKINNER'S MAIN FOCUS

Human behavior can be shaped along desired lines by means of the systematic application of reinforcement.

Skinner's Key Ideas

The model presented in this chapter is called neo-Skinnerian to indicate that it is made up of new applications of Skinner's basic ideas. Skinner himself never proposed a model of school discipline. Other writers, such as Axelrod (1977), Ladoucer and Armstrong (1983), and Sharpley (1985), have taken his ideas on learning and adapted them to controlling the behavior of students in school. The following ideas reveal the essence of the neo-Skinnerian model:

1. Behavior is shaped by its consequences, by what happens to the individual immediately afterward.
2. Systematic use of reinforcement (rewards) can shape students' behavior in desired directions.
3. Behavior becomes weaker if not followed by reinforcement.
4. Behavior is also weakened by punishment.
5. In the early stages of learning, constant reinforcement produces the best results.
6. Once learning has reached the desired level, it is best maintained through intermittent reinforcement, provided only occasionally.
7. Behavior modification is applied in these two main ways:
   a. The teacher observes the student perform a desired act; the teacher rewards the student; the student tends to repeat the act.
   b. The teacher observes the student perform an undesired act; the teacher either ignores the act or punishes the student, then praises a student who is behaving correctly; the misbehaving student becomes less likely than before to repeat the act.
8. Behavior modification successfully uses various kinds of reinforcers. They include social reinforcers such as verbal comments, facial expressions, and gestures; graphic reinforcers such as marks and stars; activity reinforcers such as free time and collaborating with a friend; and tangible reinforcers such as prizes and printed awards.

Remember that the model of discipline described in this chapter was not proposed by B. F. Skinner, but rather is a composite of his ideas and their extensions made by many people following in his footsteps. It is a powerful model for classroom teachers, one that can be easily modified and implemented with students of all ages and backgrounds. The model will be examined by: (1) considering essential terminology; (2) noting beneficial aspects of the model; (3) reemphasizing the dangers of punishment; (4) explaining various types of reinforcers; (5) exploring systems of behavior modification; (6) showing how a plan of behavior modification is formulated; and (7) showing how a plan of behavior modification is implemented.

ESSENTIAL TERMINOLOGY

Skinner established precise definitions of terms he used, such as operant behavior, reinforcing stimuli, schedules of reinforcement, successive approximations, positive reinforcement, and negative reinforcement. You must understand the meanings of these terms if you are to understand the model well. We need not be overly concerned about the exact wording of Skinner's definitions, but the fundamental concepts inherent in each are of basic importance.

Operant behavior is simply behavior that the student produces. It comes not as a response, reaction, or reflex but as purposeful voluntary action. Operant behaviors may be any of the immense variety of actions that individuals are able to perform voluntarily, such as entering the room quietly, taking a seat, completing an assignment, listening during a lesson, and so on.

Reinforcing stimuli are stimuli that the individual receives immediately after performing an operant behavior. In school they include such things as smiles, nods, praise, points, and free time. We can think of reinforcers as rewards. When we see a student exhibit any behavior (operant) that we think especially worthy of attention we can immediately give that individual a reward. Receiving the reward pleases the student, who will likely repreat the behavior. The process of supplying rewards is called *reinforcement*.

Schedules of reinforcement were important in Skinner's experimental work. Different schedules were shown to produce different effects. Constant reinforcement, provided every time a desired act is seen, is most effective in establishing new learnings. Every time all students in the class enter quietly, sit down, and look at the teacher, they are awarded a team point that goes toward earning a specific benefit at a later time. Individuals work hard and fast to earn prized rewards. Once new learning is acquired it can be maintained indefinitely by using intermittent reinforcement, in which reward is supplied only occasionally. The individual knows that reward will come sooner or later and so keeps on trying.

Successive approximations refers to a progression in which actions (operants) come closer and closer to a pre-set goal. Teachers have to work toward many learnings and behaviors in gradual ways, taking one small step at a time. Successive approximations are small-step improvements leading to the overall learning. For example, the class enters the room and sits down. There is still too much chatter but the teacher gives the class a point for improvement, in that everyone is seated. Later, the students will have to be seated and quiet to earn a point. Teachers reinforce the small improvements to help the students progress more rapidly.

Positive reinforcement is the process of supplying a reward that the student wants, something that will spur greater effort. In classrooms, teachers provide effective reinforcement by means of comments (good job; nice work), stickers, and points. For classroom purposes we need not confuse ourselves about positive and negative reinforcement. We can simply call all rewards reinforcers.

Negative reinforcement is a term that is misunderstood (and used incorrectly) by most classroom teachers. They think of negative reinforcement as meaning harsh punishment that will suppress behavior. Just the opposite is true. Negative reinforcement *increases* the likelihood of behavior, just as does positive reinforcement. Negative means taking away something that the student doesn't like, rather that adding something that the student does like. Negative reinforcement has only limited application in classrooms. Tauber (1982) illustrates the process with the following examples: "If you score 80 percent or higher on the exam you will not have to turn in a final paper." (The final paper is "taken away" as a reward for scoring well on the exam.) "If you get all of your assignments in on time . . . you will be allowed to drop your lowest grade" (p. 66). These examples show how negative reinforcement is provided through the removal of an "aversive"—something students dislike.

BENEFICIAL ASPECTS OF BEHAVIOR MODIFICATION

Since the beginning of human history, parents and teachers have used punishment to motivate learning in the young. Learners did what they were supposed to do or suffered harsh lectures or even physical punishment from their teachers. This punitive system of motivation persists to the present day and is still evident in some classrooms. But is it effective?

Skinner found in his experiments that animals worked harder and learned more quickly if given rewards for doing something right than if given punishment for doing wrong. This made sense when working with rats and pigeons because there was no way to tell them what we wanted them to do and what would happen to them if they didn't comply.

When the notion of providing rewards for desired behavior was applied to school students, an interesting fact came to light. Students, like rats and pigeons, responded better to positive rewards than they did to punishment. Of course, there were, and are, exceptions. But generally speaking, rewards spur interest and effort. Moreover, they help clarify what is expected.

Behavior modification is based almost entirely on rewards. It gives teachers power to work with students in positive ways. It lets them get away from harshness and punishment, which neither students nor teachers like. It allows them to maintain control within classroom environments that are warm, supportive, and positive, instead of cold, harsh, and punitive. This coincides with a growing trend toward humaneness in all walks of life.

Behavior modification is good for speeding the learning of academic material as well as enhancing good personal behavior. It has the advantage of allowing the teacher to work in a supportive manner, emphasizing the positive and reducing the negative. It also helps students build desired behavior. A little reward given as each step is accomplished helps spur interest and desire to behave acceptably.

THE DANGERS OF PUNISHMENT

Punishment is effective in stopping undesired behavior. It works quickly, much more quickly than positive reinforcement. When students are fighting, it is ludicrous to think of allowing the fight to continue while looking for a student who is sitting quietly so you can say "Thank you, Susan, for sitting quietly and not fighting." Instead, we do whatever is necessary to stop the fight and suppress students' inclination to continue, even if that means punishing the offenders.

Skinner did not, at first, believe that punishment weakened misbehavior. He stated that punishment could suppress misbehavior but not eradicate it. He later had to change his mind, based on experiments he conducted.

But punishment has its dark side. While it suppresses unwanted behavior, it produces side effects that sometimes override the best educational intents. If students see punishment as unwarranted, malicious, or excessive, bad feelings result that are very difficult to overcome. Those feelings may provoke retaliation toward teacher and other students, or withdrawal. Meanwhile, punishment re-teaches that might makes right.

For these reasons, teachers are advised to use punishment as little as possible, to try the positive approach first. Of course, students must know what they are doing wrong, if it is not evident to them. And they must also know how they are supposed to behave.

An effective middle ground is to use punishment depicted as the logical consequences that follow misbehavior. Students may be punished (not harshly), but only after they have previously been informed of exactly what is expected of them, what will happen when they comply, and what will happen (the logical consequences) when they do not. In this fashion, students come to understand that they themselves choose the punishment that invariably accompanies misbehavior.

TYPES OF REINFORCERS

Bear in mind that reinforcers can be anything that an individual wants badly enough to do something to earn them. They can range from such mundane things as a breath of fresh air to such rarities as Pulitzer prizes. Many of the things that students want cannot be dispensed in school, and while that puts limitations on what teachers can use as reinforcers, they still have a powerful arsenal at their disposal. Reinforcers commonly used in schools fall into four categories: social, graphic, activity, and tangible.

Social reinforcers consist of words, gestures, and facial expressions. Many students work diligently just to get a smile, pat, or kind word from the teacher. Some examples are:

Verbal
- Ok. Wow! Excellent. Nice going. Exactly. Right. Thank you. I like that. Would you share that?

Nonverbal
- Smiles, winks, eye contact, nods, thumbs up, touches, pats, walk beside, stand near, shake hands.

Graphic reinforcers include marks of various kinds, such as numerals, checks, happy faces, and special symbols. Teachers make these marks with felt pens and rubber stamps. They may enter them on charts or use a paper punch to make holes in cards kept by the students. They may attach stars or stickers that are commercially available in large quantities and varieties.

Activity reinforcers include those activities that students prefer in school. Any school activity can be used as a reinforcer if students prefer it to another. Examples of activities that usually reinforce academic learning are:

For younger students
- Being a monitor, sitting near the teacher, choosing the song, caring for the pet, sharing a pet or toy.

For middle students
- Playing a game, free reading, decorating the classroom, having extra recess time, going to an assembly.

For older students
- Working with a friend, being excused from a test, working on a special project, being excused from homework.

Tangible reinforcers are real objects that students can earn as rewards for desired behavior and are more powerful for some students than other types of reinforcers. They are widely used with students who have special behavior problems. Many elementary teachers use tangible reinforcers regularly. Examples of inexpensive reinforcers are: popcorn, raisins, chalk, crayons, felt pens, pencils, badges, decals, pennants, used books, old magazines, stationery, posters, rubber stamps, certificates, notes, letters, and plastic tokens.

SYSTEMS OF BEHAVIOR MODIFICATION

Behavior modification works even when done sporadically, but it is best approached in a systematic way. A random approach has been used for decades, based on teachers' praising students for doing good work. That fact causes many teachers to say, when behavior modification is introduced, "But I've always done that." In truth, however, few teachers in the past used reinforcement systematically as a means of shaping desired behavior. They used praise on a hit-or-miss basis. Behavior modification is maximally effective when used in an organized, systematic, and consistent manner.

Systems of behavior modification are legion. Every teacher adds a personal twist. Such flexibility is a strength because it allows teachers to apply reinforcement in ways consistent with their personalities and those of their students. The multitude of systems fit roughly into five categories: (1) informal "catch 'em being good"; (2) rules-ignore-praise (RIP); (3) rules-reward-punishment (RRP); (4) contingency management; and (5) contracting.

Catch 'Em Being Good

This approach rests solely on rewarding students who are doing what is expected. The teacher says, "Class, take out your math books." Several students get their books at once. Others waste time talking. The teacher picks out students who acted as directed and says: "Thank you, Helen, for being ready. Thank you, Ted. I like the way Ramon got his book immediately." Many other students then open their books at once and pay attention. This strategy offers two benefits. First, it reinforces the proper behavior of Helen, Ted, and Ramon, and second, it shapes behavior of other students as well.

The catch 'em being good approach is highly effective in primary grades. Teachers through third grade use it extensively. By fourth grade it begins to lose effectiveness, and by junior high students find it laughable.

Older students do, however, tend to respond well when reinforced as a group rather than being singled out individually. There are, however, still better approaches to be used with older students.

Rules-Ignore-Praise (RIP)

The RIP approach is used as follows. The teacher, perhaps with student involvement, formulates a set of rules for class behavior. The rules might be:

1. Be courteous to others.
2. Keep hands, feet, and objects to yourself.
3. Complete all assignments.
4. Work without disturbing others.
5. Follow all directions.

These rules are made very clear and understandable to the students. They made be written on a chart and posted at the front of the room. This list is kept short—five or six rules, few enough that students, with reminders, can keep them in mind.

Once the rules are established the teacher watches for people who are complying with them. She might say "Row 1 is doing an excellent job of following directions!" Students who comply with the rules receive praise, and every student is praised as often as possible. Student behavior that breaks the rules is ignored. That is, no direct attention at all is given to the student. No reinforcement comes from the teacher. Instead the teacher immediately finds a student who is following the rules and praises that student. When Mrs. Jenet sees Tim poke his neighbor, she goes to an adjacent student, Sally, who is following the rules, gives Sally a sticker, and says "Thank you Sally for working without bothering others."

This system works fairly well at the elementary level, provided that the class is relatively well-behaved to begin with. But it is not effective at the secondary level. Students speak derisively of peers who receive public praise from the teacher, calling them pets and "kiss-ups." Moreover, secondary students when misbehaving are not shaped well through praise given to others. They are already getting enough positive reinforcement in the form of peer attention, teacher attention, and laughter.

Rules-Reward-Punishment (RRP)

'The RRP approach builds limits and consequences into behavior modification. As with RIP, RRP begins with rules and emphasizes rewards, but it does not ignore inappropriate behavior. The added factor of limits and consequences makes this approach especially effective with older students and with students who have behavior problems.

The rules phase is the same as described earlier. Rules, as few in number as possible, are established, understood, and put on written display. The teacher becomes very direct about compliance. Students who follow the rules will be rewarded in various ways. They will receive praise, if appropriate. They will receive laudatory notes to take home to their parents. They will earn points that count toward a larger reward, either for the individual or for the class as a whole.

Students are clearly informed about what will happen if the rules are broken. They realize that it is their prerogative to break the rules. But if they do so, they simultaneously choose the consequences that follow and punishment is invoked immediately in accord with procedures described fully and carefully to the class. When Jane refuses to begin her work, Mr. Trammel tells her that, in accord with the rules and consequences, she must sit at the table in the rear of the room until she completes her assignment. In a sense the teacher does not punish misbehavior; students punish themselves. They have chosen to behave in ways that automatically bring undesired consequences.

This system is quite effective with older students. It clearly sets expectations, rewards, and punishments. Students consider it fair, know that they have the power to choose consequences through their behavior, and that the responsibility for good behavior rests directly on their shoulders.

Contingency Management

Mrs. Vickers explained that she uses a "token economy" in her classroom. If the students stay in their seats, raise their hands, finish their work, and so on, she rewards them with plastic chips. The chips can be exchanged later for desired rewards.

Mrs. Vickers' plan is an example of contingency management, which involves an elaborate system of tangible reinforcers. It has been used widely with all types of students at kindergarten through high school. It has been shown to be especially effective for working with behavior-problem students and with the mentally retarded.

Sometimes referred to as token economies, contingency management systems use tokens that students earn for desired behaviors such as staying in their seats, raising their hands, finishing their work, improving over past performance, and so forth. The tokens may be exchanged for tokens of higher value or cashed in for prizes such as food, toys, comic books, magazines, badges, privileges, and other activities. In actual practice, teachers find that the tokens often become sufficiently rewarding in themselves. Students have no desire to cash them in, preferring simply to amass and possess the tokens. Plastic discs and poker chips are often used for tokens. Some teachers print up play money in different denominations, as well as special certificates of various types.

Teachers who use token economies must be sure to award the tokens fairly and consistently. They must have an adequate supply of tokens, provide a manageable way for students to keep their tokens, and be sure that counterfeiting and extortion do not occur. They must set aside a time every few weeks for students to cash in their tokens. Students can buy "white elephants" that other students have brought from home, the teacher can obtain free materials from various shops and stores, and vouchers can be made for special activities and privileges. Each object and voucher has its price in tokens. Some teachers like to have auctions in which students bid for the items available.

Teachers who use this plan should explain it very carefully to the principal, the students, and the parents before putting it into practice. This ensures that everyone approves and understands what is taking place, thus preventing objections that are otherwise likely to occur.

Contracting

The use of contracts has been widespread and successful, especially at the intermediate and secondary levels. Contracts specify work to be done or behavior to be established, with deadlines for completion. They indicate what the payoff will be for successful accomplishment, and they indicate what input the teacher will give. They lend an air of legality, promise, and responsibility. Student and teacher both sign the agreement. Sometimes parents cosign with the student.

Mr. Lex has a contract with Jesse, who has been continually remiss in bringing needed materials to class. Jesse has agreed to bring paper, pencil, and textbook to class every day. If he does this five days in a row, he gets five points. When he has accumulated 15 points he can exchange them for a special pen from Mr. Lex's collection.

Contract forms can be prepared and duplicated in quantity. For older students quasi-legal terminology adds a pleasing touch, as do filigree and official stamps of gold foil or contact paper. While contracts are fun to use, they must be seen as serious commitments, the terms of which must be lived up to by all who have signed.

PLANNING AND IMPLEMENTING
BEHAVIOR MODIFICATION

Teachers who intend to use behavior modification need to spend some time planning in advance. According to various experts, the planning should focus on two things: (1) analysis of the behaviors one wants to change, and (2) development of a specific plan to change those behaviors.

Analysis consists of identifying the behaviors to be changed or improved, deciding what is wrong with them at present, and determining what they should be in the future. It should include consideration of *antecedents*, conditions in the classroom that encourage misbehavior, and *consequences*, the system of rewards and punishments that will be used to motivate and guide student behavior. Antecedents include such factors as distractions, boredom, poor models, awkward transitions between lessons, and so forth. Consequences include, as reinforcers, any of the many factors already described in this chapter as well as the logical-consequence punishers that suppress misbehavior. This analysis may at first appear to be a complicated process, but in fact it can be done adequately within a few minutes.

Implementation refers to formulating the behavior modification plan and putting it into practice. The plan follows from the analysis of behavior and the identification of desired reinforcers and punishers. It may be written in outline form, providing reminders of specific things to be done, and it can be used jointly by teachers and students.

Target behaviors are the new behaviors that one wishes to see exhibited by students. Systematic reinforcement shapes classroom behavior in the direction of those targets. If a target behavior is to prevent students from talking out in class wtihout permission, the teacher might reward people who raise their hands and wait to be called on before they speak. Verbal praise can be used for reinforcement, such as, "Thank you, Maria, for raising your hand." If the target behavior is to stay on task for the entire work period, reinforcements are given for that behavior. Reinforcement is given very frequently at first, and as the behavior improves rewards are given less frequently.

The implementation plan calls for correcting antecedent conditions that might be contributing to poor behavior, things such as uncertainty about rules, forgetfulness, poor peer models, inadequate teacher models, awkward times between lessons, poor lesson pacing, boredom, frustration, and lack of interesting activities for students. Removal of such conditions gives the behavior modification plan a much greater chance of success.

Students who chronically misbehave do so in part because their misbehavior is bringing them some type of reinforcement. These reinforcers might include teacher and peer attention, laughter, sense of power, getting one's own way, etc. This pattern must be changed so that misbehavior brings negative consequences rather than positive ones. Negative consequences range from ignoring (by both teacher and students) to isolation from the group. Positive consequences meanwhile must be supplied for desired behavior. Teachers can always find someone doing what they are supposed to do. Teachers identify that person by name (at primary grade levels) and tell what the person was doing right. At secondary levels, teachers reinforce the behavior anonymously, for example: "Class, I really appreciate the way many of you helped us get started by having your work ready."

Students can also learn to reinforce themselves, a tactic that can be quite powerful. Suggestions for self-reward have been put forth by several authorities. For example, Ogden Lindsley ("Precision Teaching," 1971) described a technique called precision teaching that involves graphing student performance, whether academic or personal behavior. The graph documents performance, but it has a great additional advantage: Students can graph their own performance, greatly increasing their interest in improving. With each improved mark, they reinforce their own behavior.

Another example of student self-reinforcement comes from Mahoney and Thoresen (1972), who described a system in which students set up their own systems of reward and punishment, which they apply as consequences to their own behavior. Kindergarten students who finish their artwork may go on their own to the play area. Fifth graders who have not disrupted for the entire math period may go to the reinforcement area and pick up a permit for 10 minutes of free reading. Secondary students who complete assignments accurately before they are due allow themselves to work together with a friend.

Self-rewarding is of course subject to misuse. Students will not always earn the reinforcement they select. In this event, teachers must first inspect the student's work or behavior, then signal an okay for the reinforcement. The student then selects the reinforcer.

BEHAVIOR MOD FOREVER

Teachers who once begin using behavior modification in a systematic way rarely stop. They appreciate its powerful effects. They come to see it not as manipulating students but as freeing them to behave in ways that bring success and positive recognition. Systematic attention and reinforcing become natural parts of the teaching act, occurring automatically. After a while teachers do not even have to think of them. That natural spontaneity makes reinforcement even more effective. Students feel that the teacher is simply kind, considerate, and friendly, not designing or manipulative.

Teachers like what works; behavior modification does. It helps students and it makes teaching easier and more enjoyable. If you asked teachers to name the single most valuable technique for controlling and shaping student behavior, many would certainly say, "Behavior mod. Give me behavior mod forever."

Application Exercises

We continue with repetition of the Kris and Tom cases.

CASE #1. KRIS WILL NOT WORK:

Kris, in Mr. Jake's class, is quite docile. She never disrupts class and does little socializing with other students. But despite all his efforts, Mr. Jake can hardly get Kris to participate in class activities. She rarely completes an assignment. She is simply there, like a bump on a log, putting forth no effort.

How would Skinner deal with Kris? Skinner would suggest that Mr. Jake try the following approaches with Kris.

1. Catch Kris being good (doing anything that is appropriate). Reward her whenever she participates or works.
2. Reiterate the class rules regarding work. Praise Kris whenever she follows the rule.
3. Consider stronger reinforcers. If praise is ineffective, use points, tokens, or other tangible objects to reinforce and shape Kris's improvement.
4. Set up a contract with Kris. Identify a reward that is exceptionally attractive to her. Outline what she must do in order to earn the reward. Share the contract with Kris's parents to enlist their support. Reinforce every improvement Kris makes.

CASE #2. TOM IS HOSTILE AND DEFIANT:

Tom has appeared to be in his usual foul mood ever since arriving in class. He gets up and on his way to sharpen his pencil he bumps into Frank. Frank complains. Tom tells him loudly to shut up. Miss Baines, the teacher, says "Tom, go back to your seat." Tom wheels around, swears loudly and says heatedly "I'll go when I'm damned good and ready!"

How would Skinner have Miss Baines deal with Tom?

QUESTIONS AND ACTIVITIES:

1. In general terms, how would effective systems of behavior modification differ between primary grades and high school?
2. Ms. Wong is having problems in her classroom. The students enter boisterously and take a long time to settle down. They call out answers and make smart remarks during the lessons. Many do not pay attention when Ms. Wong is talking. Describe how you would set up a behavior modification system with Ms. Wong's class. (You may prepare it as if Ms. Wong's class were a first-, sixth-, or tenth-grade class.)
3. Describe how you would create an effective contract with a student (you choose the grade level) who is chronically tardy to class.

REFERENCES

Axelrod, S. (1977). *Behavior modification for the classroom teacher.* New York: McGraw-Hill.

Firth, G. (1985). *Behavior management in the schools: a primer for parents.* New York: Thomas.

Ladoucer, R., & Armstrong, J. (1983). Evaluation of a behavioral program for the improvement of grades among high school students. *Journal of Counseling Psychology 30*, 100–103.

Mahoney, M., & Thoresen, C. (1972), Behavioral self-control—power to the person, *Educational Researcher, 1*, 5–7.

Precision teaching in perspective: an interview with Ogden R. Lindsley (1971). *Teaching Exceptional Children, 3*, 114–119.

Sharpley, C. (1985). Implicit rewards in the classroom. *Contemporary Educational Psychology, 10*, 349–68.

Skinner, B. F. (1948). *Walden Two.* New York: Macmillan.

Skinner, B. F. (1971). *Beyond freedom and dignity.* New York: Knopf.

Tauber, R. (1982). Negative reinforcement: a positive strategy in classroom management. *Clearing House, 56*, 64–67.

CHAPTER 4

The Ginott Model:

Addressing the Situation with Sane Messages

GINOTT BIOGRAPHICAL SKETCH

Haim Ginott was born in Tel Aviv, Israel, in 1922. He earned his PhD at Columbia University in 1952 and went on to become a professor of psychology at New York University Graduate School and a professor of psychology at Adelphi University. He also served in Israel as a UNESCO consultant, was a resident psychologist on television's "Today Show," and wrote a weekly syndicated column entitled "Between Us," that dealt with interpersonal communication.

Among educators, Ginott is best known for three books that dealt with relationships between adults and the young. In the first two, *Between Parent and Child* (1965) and *Between Parent and Teenager* (1969), he offered solutions to communication breakdowns that occur between parents and their offspring. He believed that adults vitally impact children's self-esteem through the messages they send. In an attempt to make that impact positive, he developed specific skills for dealing with parent-child conflicts. As a fundamental principle, Ginott emphasized addressing the situation while avoiding attacks on the child's character. He urged parents to show their offspring that they still like them even when they disapprove of their children's behavior.

In a later book, *Teacher and Child* (1971), Ginott showed how those ideas are extended to the classroom. Teachers, like parents, hold the power to make or break a child's self-concept. *Teacher and Child* deals with methods of communication that maintain a secure, humanitarian, and productive classroom environment.

Dr. Ginott died on November 4, 1973.

GINOTT'S MAIN FOCUS

Discipline is a series of little victories, brought about when teachers use *sane massages*—messages that address the situation rather than the students' character—to guide students away from inappropriate behavior toward behavior that is appropriate and lasting.

Ginott's Key Ideas

The following is a list of key ideas advocated in Ginott's model of discipline. The remainder of the chapter elaborates on these ideas.

1. Discipline is a series of little victories, not something that occurs overnight.

2. The most important ingredient in classroom discipline is the teacher's own self-discipline.

3. The second most important ingredient is using sane messages when correcting misbehaving students. Sane message are messages that address the situation and do not attack students' characters.

4. Teachers at their best use *congruent communication*, communication that is harmonious with students' feelings about situations and themselves.

5. Teachers at their worst attack and label students' characters.

6. Teachers should model the behavior they hope to see in their students.

7. Inviting cooperation from students is vastly preferable to demanding it.

8. Teachers should express anger but in appropriate (sane) ways.

9. Labeling students disables them—they tend to live up to the label.

10. Sarcasm is almost always dangerous, and praise is often dangerous. Use both with great care.

11. Apologies from students should be accepted with the understanding that students intend to improve.

12. The best teachers help students to build their own self-esteem and to trust their own experience.

THE GINOTT MODEL OF DISCIPLINE

Teachers are a decisive, powerful element in the classroom. They create and maintain the environment. They have the power to humanize or dehumanize their students. Their effectiveness depends on their ability to establish an educational climate that promotes optimal learning. Children who are in constant emotional turmoil cannot learn. To reduce this turmoil, Ginott advocates using *congruent communication*, a harmonious and authentic way of talking in which teacher messages to students match the students' feelings about situations and themselves.

Ginott claims that the principle of congruent communication is the crucial factor in classroom climate. Teachers must constantly endeavor to use it. When they do so, they convey an attitude of helpfulness and acceptance and are continually aware of the impact of their messages on students' self-esteem. Congruent communication incorporates many different elements that we see expressed in Ginott's descriptions of teachers at their best and at their worst.

Teachers at Their Best

Ginott wrote at length about teachers at their best and at their worst. At their best, teachers use congruent communication, evidenced when they:

1. Send sane messages, addressing the situation rather than the student's character.
2. Express anger appropriately.
3. Invite cooperation.
4. Accept and acknowledge student feelings.
5. Avoid labeling students.
6. Correct students by directing them appropriately.
7. Avoid the perils of praise.
8. Are brief when correcting students.
9. Are models of humane behavior.

Teachers at Their Worst

Teachers at their worst fail to use congruent communication, as shown when they:

1. Are caustic and sarcastic.
2. Attack students' characters.
3. Demand, rather than invite, cooperation.
4. Deny students' feelings.
5. Label students as lazy, stupid, and so forth.
6. Give long and unnecessary lectures.
7. Lose their tempers and self-control.
8. Use praise to manipulate students.
9. Are poor models of humane behavior.

Let us look futher at some of Ginott's suggestions for helping teachers function at their best.

Sane Messages

Sane messages address situations rather than students' characters. They *accept and acknowledge* how students feel. Sanity, according to Ginott, depends on people's ability to trust their own perception of reality. Too often, adults send insane messages, telling the young to distrust or deny their feelings or inner reality. They blame, preach, command, accuse, belittle, and threaten. In so doing, they tell children to deny their feelings about themselves and to build their feelings of self-worth from the judgments of others.

Ginott (1973) repeatedly reiterates his cardinal principle of the sane message. When a student gets in trouble the teacher should always address the situation and never judge the student's character or personality. *By simply describing the scene of concern*, teachers allow students to appraise the situation, consider what is right and wrong, and decide how they feel about the situation and themselves.

Here is an example of a sane message: Two students are talking during a quiet time, violating class rules. The teacher says, "This is a quiet time. It needs to be absolutely silent." An insane message, by contrast, might be: "You two are being very rude. You have no consideration for others who are trying to work."

Ginott maintained that teachers' manners of talking with students reveal how they truly feel about them. Their ways of responding to students can build or destroy self-concept. Poor teacher responses can contradict a student's perception of self. Good teacher responses simply state the facts, letting students decide for themselves if their behavior is in keeping with what they expect of themselves.

Expressing Anger

Teaching is a tough job. Fatigue, frustration, and conflict make teacher anger inevitable. Most people, adults and students alike, expect teachers to be saints. Ginott maintained that such expectations are wrong and even damaging to teachers. Teachers should never deny human feelings, either their students' or their own. Their behavior should always be genuine. That includes how they talk, behave, and respond to students. However, they need to learn to express anger, even displeasure, without damaging the students' character.

When situations arise that cause teachers to feel angry, they should simply (and sanely) describe what they see. They should address the situation and tell how they feel about it. When they need to tell how they feel, Ginott (1972) says they should use *I-messages*. "I am angry." "I am disappointed." These I-messages are much more appropriate expressions of anger than are you-messages: "You are not being good." "You are messy." "You only think of yourself." I-messages tell how the teacher feels about the situation. You-messages attack the student.

When angry, good teachers state their demands clearly and firmly, avoiding language that insults or humiliates. Their messages are as brief as possible. It is important that teachers be good models of civilized behavior. When tempted to explode with wrath, they should ask themselves, "Am I dealing with anger in the same way I expect my students to? Am I modeling behavior I want to see replicated in my classroom?"

One last item about expressing anger: Ginott points out that an anger situation is one of those times when teachers have the full attention of students. The situation affords an opportunity to enrich vocabulary by expressing anger in eloquent terms, such as "I am appalled, indignant, chagrined. I see inexcusable and intolerable behavior. I wish to terminate the situation at once." The teacher conveys two messages, one about the students' behavior and another about the power of descriptive language. Ginott notes that using words that students understand only vaguely increases the shock value of teacher expressions of anger.

Inviting Cooperation

Ginott urges teachers to invite cooperation rather than demand it. One of the ways to issue the invitation is to decide with the class before an activity is started what kinds of personal behavior are required during the activity. Another is to stop an activity that has gotten out of control and say, "We can watch the movie in silence, or we can do another math assignment. You decide." If the students continue to disrupt, the teacher must follow through with the alternative, making it clear that such was the students' decision.

Teachers who do not invite cooperation must use ordering, bossing, and commanding. Ginott stresses the need to avoid direct commands, which frequently induce hostility. Again, Ginott says to describe the situation and let students decide what their course of action should be. Too often, teachers use long, drawn-out directions or explanations such as: "Close your library books. Put them in your desks. Get out your math book. Get a pencil. Turn to page 60. Start on the assignment." Ginott suggests a simple declaration such as, "It is now math time. The assignment is on page 60." With that kind of message, teachers show that they respect students' ability to behave autonomously. They invite cooperation, promote self-choice, and foster responsibility. Self-image improves through independent choice of productive behavior.

By inviting cooperation, teachers begin to break down students' dependency on the teacher. Of course we all depend on others in many ways, but if that dependency is too strong it creates problems. This is certainly true when students are made too dependent on teachers, as strong dependency often makes students lethargic and indecisive, even resentful and hostile. Ginott recommends reducing dependency problems by providing many opportunities for students to behave independently. One of the ways suggested by Ginott is to present students with several possible solutions to a problem and let them decide on the one they want to adopt. This helps them feel they have some control over happenings in the classroom. They can also decide how they want to proceed in applying the solution they have chosen. Given these opportunities to make decisions, they come to depend less on the teacher for motivation and direction. Also, they are more likely to live up to standards of behavior they have set for themselves.

Accepting and Acknowledging Feelings

Students are in an awkward position in that they recognize they have their own feelings about themselves and about situations, but at the same time are also told how they *should* feel by adults. Ginott believes teachers can be especially useful in helping students sort out feelings. He would like for teachers to minimize student confusion by withholding their opinions and merely acting as sounding boards for students with problems.

Consider young children as an example. Their perceptions of reality are much different from those of adults. Youngsters routinely exaggerate the truth, and their opinions often have little basis in reality. Teachers should not argue with children's perceptions, even when they are obviously wrong. This only causes feelings of belittlement and rejection. Instead, teachers should strive to acknowledge and understand children's feelings.

Here is an example: Suppose Juan comes running in from the playground crying, "Jose threw a ball at me and hit me in the head on purpose. Everyone started laughing at me. No one likes me." The teacher could argue with the child's experience and deny his feelings, saying "That's silly. I'm sure it was an accident. The others were laughing at something else." Or she could respond with sympathy and understanding, offering no judgment on the situation, saying "You seem very upset. You feel that no one likes you. Your feelings are hurt when others laugh at you." In this way, the child's feelings are acknowledged and respected. He is not put on the defensive or told how he should feel.

Ginott suggests that teachers add another comment to such situations: "How can I help you?" This provides an opportunity for the student to come up with a solution to the problem and reveals the teacher's confidence in the student's ability to cope. By acknowledging feelings and offering to be helpful, the teacher does not deny feelings, reject opinions, attack a student's character, or argue with the student's experience. Students must have an opportunity to decide how they feel and what they are going to do about it.

Children's fears are another matter that should be treated carefully. Adults have the tendency to make light of them. When they do this, they tell children that their feelings are not real. Adults also may cause them to believe that people are not supposed to feel that way. Ginott says to avoid the standard adult phrase, "There is nothing to be afraid of," which only makes children feel worse. They are now stuck with both the original fear and a new fear of showing fear. Telling children not to be afraid, angry, or sad does not dispel those emotions, but it does cause them to doubt their own inner feelings. It causes them to doubt the teacher's ability to understand and teaches them that adults are not to be trusted during times of trouble.

Labeling Is Disabling

Teachers are sometimes heard to make statements to students such as, "You're lazy, irresponsible, and sloppy. You'll never amount to anything if you don't change." By now you realize that Ginott is adamant about there being no place in the classroom for such labels, diagnoses, or prognoses of students' character.

Labeling is disabling, Ginott avows, because it tells students how to think about themselves. When subjected to these messages often enough they begin to believe them. They start to live up to a negative self-image. This is especially true when adults attempt to predict a student's future. When teachers tell students to forget about going to college they may do just that. The very art of teaching demands that teachers open vistas, encourage growth and achievement, provide enlightenment, and stimulate imagination. Labeling and diagnosing a student's character only limits visions of the self and the future.

In difficult situations, teachers can avoid labeling while striving to be helpful and encouraging. They can offer statements like, "Your grades are low, but I know if we work together we can improve them." "You want to be veterinarian? Did you know there is a career information section in the media center?" Statements such as these do not tell students what you think they can or cannot do. They encourage students to set goals for themselves and they assure them that the teacher will support and assist in the attainment of those goals. When teachers believe in students, the students begin to believe in themselves.

Correction Is Direction

Throughout every day, situations arise in the classroom that require correcting comments from the teacher. Tim and Mary may throw erasers. A group of boys may discuss baseball instead of doing seatwork. Brian may stare out the window instead of completing his math assignment. In these situations Ginott recommends directing as the method of correcting.

When correcting by directing, teachers describe the situation and offer acceptable alternative behaviors. Often students simply need to be told what they could be doing differently. In the case of Tim and Mary the teacher might say, "Erasers are not for throwing. This is reading time."

When correcting misbehavior, teachers should avoid attacking a student's character. They should not rant and rave about what they dislike in it. When teachers tell what they see and suggest acceptable alternatives, students know how the teacher feels about the current behavior and exactly how they are supposed to behave differently. They become more likely to follow the teacher's suggestions and correct their own behavior.

Sarcasm

Ginott has a word of advice for teachers who are tempted to use sarcasm in the classroom—don't. Many adults use sarcasm as a form of wit. Teachers often do so with students intending only to be clever and witty. All too often, however, their sarcasm sounds clever only to themselves and not to the students receiving the comments, who end up with hurt feelings and damaged self-esteem. Students often do not understand the sarcasm and feel that they are being made fun of or belittled. It is better to avoid sarcasm altogether than to risk hurting feelings.

The Perils of Praise

Who would ever think that praise could damage a student's self-concept? Don't we all need to be told we are great, terrific, valuable? Ginott makes some provocative observations about praise. He does not deny its value, but he sees a danger there too. The danger is that teachers can use it to manipulate students' feelings about themselves. As with negative comments, praise can have detrimental effects on forming a positive self-image, especially if the praise is *judgmental*. Such praise—"You are a good boy!"—creates a dependence on others for approval and validation of self-worth.

Again, Ginott is emphatic about the importance of describing the circumstances and letting a student decide what behavior is appropriate. When praising, teachers need to concentrate on applauding *specific acts* without including adjectives about the personality.

An example of Ginott's point is seen in these comments that Mrs. Richards wrote on her student's paper: "This is an exceptional description of human emotions. This paper truly has poetic qualities." She did not make the mistake of attributing qualities of the paper to the student's personality. Instead, she allowed the student to come to his own conclusions about himself from the comments on the paper.

Another way teachers use praise inappropriately is by telling students that they are good because they know the correct answer. A logical conclusion could then be drawn by other students—that they are bad because they do not know the answer. Ginott say: "Knowledge does not make one good. The lack of it does not make one bad." Appropriate responses for correct answers are "fine," "exactly," or "that's correct." These comments carry no evaluation of the student's personality.

Praising good behavior can have its drawbacks, too. When teachers praise students for behavior they are supposed to show, it may apear that the teacher is surprised by good behavior, implying that poor behavior is expected. Sometimes students decide to live up to negative expectations.

Teachers should express their feelings of appreciation without words that evalute the students' behavior. Ginott would have the teacher say, "Thank you for entering quietly," or "I enjoyed working with you today." He would not want them to say "You were so good at the assembly," or "You can really behave when you want to." Ginott insists that evaluative praise inevitably puts teachers in a judgmental position. It causes them to appear condescending. Persons on a higher status level are at liberty to praise those on lower level, but not vice versa. Students would seem disrespectful if they said, "You can do a fine job, Mr. Green, when you really want to."

Another danger that should be recognized in evaluative praise is that it so easily manipulates student behavior. When teachers give profuse praise they are trying to ensure repetition of a desired behavior. Students, especially older ones, sometimes resist such obvious manipulation. They feel that the praise is not sincere, but is only delivered to coerce them into certain behavior.

On the other hand, praise correctly used can be productive. Such is the case when teachers describe their own feelings or describe the efforts of students, for example, "It makes me feel good to see such quality work," or "The amount of work that has gone into this drawing is obvious." These are honest recognitions without value judgments about the students' personalities. In summary, praise well used supports, motivates, and encourages; it does not judge people. Teachers should use it to recognize effort and show apreciation, while letting students make their own evaluations about themselves.

GINOTT'S SPECIAL VIEWS ON DISCIPLINE

Ginott describes discipline as "a series of little victories. It is not one thing that a teacher does one time. It is a small step, ongoing, never ending. When done properly, it ultimately produces student self-direction, responsibility, and concern for others.

Of course, teachers can influence student behavior through threats and punishment, which generate ill will, rebellion, and subversion. Or, they can influence behavior through compassion and understanding, which can turn volatile situations into victories for students and teacher alike.

Students often misbehave in order to get reactions from adults, who almost always react negatively. These negative reactions support students' negative opinions of themselves and also their opinions of adults. Good teachers talk and act in ways that do not confirm negative expectations.

Ginott states that the most important ingredient of effective discipline is the teacher's own self-discipline. Teachers with self-discipline do not lose their tempers, insult others, or resort to name calling. They are not rude, sadistic, or unreasonable. Rather, they strive to model the behavior they expect of their students. They are polite, helpful, and respectful. They handle conflict calmly and reasonably. In the face of crisis, they show civilized behavior. Students continually watch to see how teachers handle difficult situations, and not surprisingly tend to imitate them.

Ginott presents many vignettes on discipline that describe disciplinary methods that are inappropriate as well as those that are appropriate. To begin with the negative, he asserts that teachers using inappropriate discipline:

1. Lose their tempers. (Shout, slam books, use verbal abuse.)
2. Call students names. ("You are like pigs! Clean that up!")
3. Insult students' character. ("John, you are nothing but lazy!")
4. Behave rudely. ("Sit down and shut up!")
5. Overreact. (When Mary accidentally drops a sheaf of papers being handed out: "Oh for heaven's sake! Can't you do anything right?!!")
6. Show cruelty. ("Watch carefully on your way home from school, Jack. You're a little short on brains.")
7. Punish all for the sins of one. ("Since certain people couldn't listen during the assembly, we will all have to miss the next one.")
8. Threaten. ("If I hear one more voice, we will all stay 10 minutes after school.")
9. Deliver long lectures. ("It has come to my attention that several students think the trash can is a basketball hoop. We can throw things out on the grounds, but in the classroom...etc., etc.")
10. Back students into a corner. ("What are you doing? Why are you doing that? Don't you know any better? Apologize at once!")
11. Make arbitrary rules. (Rules are made without any student input or discussion.)

In contrast, teachers who use appropriate discipline:

1. Recognize feelings. ("I can see that you are angry because you have to stay after school.")
2. Describe the situation. ("I can see coats all over the closet floor. They need to be hung up.")

3. Invite cooperation. ("Let's all help to be quiet, so we can go to the performance.")
4. Are brief. ("We do not throw paper.")
5. Do not argue. (They stick to a decision, but remain flexible enough to change it if they are wrong. Arguing is always a losing proposition for teachers.)
6. Model appropriate behavior. (They show through example how they want students to behave.)
7. Discourage physical violence. ("In our class we talk about our problems. We do not hit, kick, or pull hair.")
8. Do not criticize, call names, or insult. (A student interrupts the teacher. Teacher: "Excuse me. I will be with you as soon as I can.")
9. Focus on solutions. ("I am seeing unsportsmanlike conduct here. What can we do about that?")
10. Allow face-saving exits. ("You may remain at your desk and read quietly, or you may sit by yourself in the back of the room.")
11. Allow students to help set standards. ("What do we need to remember when we are using this paint?")
12. Are helpful. (Mathew yells, "Roger and Joe are teasing me!" Teacher responds, "You sound upset. What would you like me to do?")
13. De-escalate conflicts. (Susan, crumpling her paper: "I'm not going to do this assignment! It's too hard!" Teacher: "You feel this assignment is too difficult. Would you like me to go over a few problems with you?")

COMMENT ON GINOTT'S VIEWS

Ginott believes it is the teacher's job to provide an environment conducive to learning. An important part of this environment is the social-emotional atmosphere in the classroom. He believes that discipline problems will diminish markedly if teachers show concern for students' feelings and recognize that their messages have strong impact on students' feelings and self-esteem.

His suggestions for congruent communication are similar in some ways to Kounin's "withitness." When teachers address the situation rather than the student's character, they communicate that: (1) they know what is going on, (2) they know what they want changed, and (3) they are aware of the student's feelings.

But far more than the models considered previously, Ginott's model emphasizes how teachers should deal positively with students' emotions and exemplify good behavior in their own personal conduct.

To a far greater extent than most authorities, Ginott reminds teachers that students are people, too. Being bossed or labeled gives students justification for distrusting adults and being rebellious. Teachers should treat students as they themselves would like to be treated—by giving them choices, being helpful, and inviting rather than demanding cooperation. They should ask themselves, "How do I want my students to relate to me and each other, and how should I treat them in order that they will do so?"

Most teachers will obtain better behavior from students, and will enjoy teaching more, if they incorporate Ginott's suggestions into their teaching styles. However, even after becoming adept in the techniques Ginott advocates, many teachers find that still more is required when they must face hostile, defiant students who refuse to work or behave properly. While they have great sympathy with Ginott, most teachers conclude that for hard-to-manage classes, Ginott's suggestions do not provide all the help that teachers need.

Application Exercises

CASE #1. KRIS WILL NOT WORK:

Kris, a student in Mr. Jake's class, is quite docile. She does little socializing with other students and never disrupts class. Mr. Jake simply cannot get her to do her work. She never completes an assignment, but just sits there like a bump on a log, putting forth no effort at all.

How would Ginott deal with Kris? Ginott would advise teachers to use a number of gentle tactics to encourage Kris to do her work. These would include:

- Sane messages (Students in my class are expected to complete all assignments.)
- Inviting cooperation (All students who finish their work can then choose to play a game with a friend.)
- Accepting and acknowledging Kris's feelings (Kris, I can tell you find it difficult to begin work on your assignment. How can I help you?)
- Correct by directing (You need to finish 10 problems within the next 30 minutes.)
- Focus on solutions (This cannot continue. What do you think we might be able to do about it?)

CASE #2. TOM IS HOSTILE AND DEFIANT:

Tom has appeared to be in his usual foul mood ever since arriving in class. He gets up and on his way to sharpen his pencil he bumps into Frank. Frank complains. Tom tells him loudly to shut up. Miss Baines, the teacher, says "Tom, go back to your seat." Tom wheels around, swears loudly and says heatedly "I'll go when I'm damned good and ready!"

How would Ginott advise Miss Baines to deal with Tom?

QUESTIONS AND ACTIVITIES:

1. The following statements illustrate some of Ginott's main points about talking with students. Identify the main point with which each statement is associated.
   a) You boys head the list of my all-time laziest students.
   b) Yes, I'm just *sure* you didn't do your assignment because your mother was sick last night.
   c) I am so disappointed and angry I could pop!
   d) Alicia, you are the most intelligent kid I have ever known!
2. Peggy and June are each accusing the other of taking personal items without permission. What would Ginott have the teacher say to the girls?
3. Miss Tykes is dealing with a group of boys who were shouting obscenities in the hall. "That's the worst thing I have ever witnessed!" she yells. "Where do you think you are? Are you allowed to behave like hoodlums at home? You will all report to my room after school for the next two weeks!" How would Ginott advise that Miss Tykes change her approach?

REFERENCES

Ginott, H. (1965). *Between parent and child*. New York: Avon.

Ginott, H. (1969). *Between parent and teenager*. New York: Macmillan.

Ginott, H. (1971). *Teacher and child*. New York: Macmillan.

Ginott, H. (1972). I am angry! I am appalled! I am furious! *Today's Education, 61*, 23–24.

Ginott, H. (1973). Driving children sane. *Today's Education, 62*, 20–25.

CHAPTER 5

The Dreikurs Model:

Confronting Mistaken Goals

DREIKURS BIOGRAPHICAL SKETCH

Rudolf Dreikurs was born in Vienna, Austria, on February 8, 1897. After receiving his medical degree from the University of Vienna he entered into a long association with the renowned psychiatrist, Alfred Adler. Their studies dealt with family and child counseling. Dreikurs immigrated to the United States in 1937 and eventually became director of the Alfred Adler Institute in Chicago. He also served as professor of psychiatry at the Chicago Medical School. Throughout his career, he continued to focus on family-child counseling. He became known as an expert in the area of classroom behavior through his books *Psychology in the Classroom* (1968), *Discipline Without Tears* with P. Cassel (1972), and *Maintaining Sanity in the Classroom* with B. Grunwald and F. Pepper (1982). These books are valuable to teachers for their explanations of the motivations behind student behavior. Dr. Dreikurs died on May 31, 1972.

DREIKURS' MAIN FOCUS

All students want recognition, and most misbehavior occurs from their attempts to get it. When unable to get the recognition they desire, their behavior turns toward four "mistaken goals," which teachers must recognize and deal with.

Dreikurs' Key Ideas

1. Discipline is not punishment. It is teaching students to impose limits on themselves.
2. Democratic teachers provide firm guidance and leadership. They allow students to have a say in establishing rules and consequences.
3. All students want to belong. They want status and recognition. Most of their behaviors indicate efforts to belong.
4. Misbehavior reflects the mistaken belief that it will gain students the recognition they want.
5. Misbehavior is associated with four mistaken goals: attention getting, power seeking, revenge seeking, and displaying inadequacy.
6. Teachers should identify mistaken goals and then act in ways that do not reinforce them.
7. Teachers should strive to encourage students' efforts, but avoid praising their work or character.
8. Teachers should teach students that unpleasant consequences will always follow inappropriate behavior.

THE NATURE OF DISCIPLINE

Discipline is essential to smooth functioning in schools and society. Too often, adults have an either-or concept of discipline—*either* children behave *or* they walk all over you. Most people think of discipline as punishing actions used against children in times of conflict or misbehavior.

Children form stereotyped ideas about discipline, too. Generally, they see it as arbitrary rules set up by adults to show who is in charge. They may view discipline as a complex game with rules they do not understand. Some see it as punishment given without reason. These children soon decide that being punished justifies retaliation, rebellion, and hostility.

Good discipline, however, has little to do with punishment. Punishment is physical pain, humiliation, isolation, and revenge; it is a force imposed on one from an outside source. Dreikurs claims that "it teaches what not to do, but fails to teach what to do."

Discipline requires freedom of choice and the understanding of consequences. It is not imposed by authority figures, but rather on individuals by themselves. By choosing to behave in certain ways individuals learn to gain acceptance from others and, consequently, acceptance of themselves.

Discipline in the classroom means setting limits for students until they are able to set limits for themselves. It involves allowing students freedom to choose their own behavior. They can do this because they understand exactly what consequences will follow any behavior chosen. Good behavior brings rewards. Poor behavior *always* brings undesired consequences. When teachers teach this concept to students they are teaching students to behave in ways that are acceptable to society. This helps students promote their own welfare in all situations.

Teaching self-discipline requires a positive, accepting atmosphere. Students must feel the teacher likes and respects them. They must understand that the teacher wants what is best for them. Students must also be allowed input into establishing rules and consequences. They should always understand the reasons for rules because this allows a sense of personal commitment and involvement. It provides recognition of the need for limits.

Dreikurs believes that establishing discipline in the classroom must involve teaching the following concepts:

1. Students are responsible for their own actions.
2. Students must respect themselves and others.
3. Students have the responsibility to influence others to behave appropriately.
4. Students are responsible for knowing what the rules and consequences are in their classrooms.

Dreikurs also believes that teachers who are most effective in establishing discipline are those who teach democratically. Let us explore the qualities of different types of teachers.

TYPES OF TEACHERS

Dreikurs identifies three types of teachers—*autocratic*, *permissive*, and *democratic*—so categorized on the basis of behavior they show in the classroom.

Autocratic Teachers

Mr. Parrons strides into the classroom in a suit and tie. His back is ramrod straight. He coldly eyes the class, then begins the lesson without a greeting. He thwarts questions by ridiculing the first student who dares to ask.

Such autocratic teachers force their will on students to prove they have control of the class. They motivate students with outside pressure instead of stimulating motivation from within. They need to feel powerful and sense superiority over students. This attitude and approach tend to perpetuate problem behavior. More and more, students reject authority figures. They seek a democratic atmosphere in which they are treated as human beings and react with hostility to the autocratic teacher.

Permissive Teachers

Mrs. Samuels smiles tentatively as she enters. Several students are not seated but she does not address them. Instead, she says, "You may visit quietly while you are working." Soon a deafening roar fills the classroom, but from her desk Mrs. Samuels seems oblivious.

Such permissive teachers are also ineffective. They, too, generate problem behavior because the atmosphere they allow is not based on everyday reality. Students in a permissive classroom do not learn that living in society requires following rules. They do not learn that failure to follow rules results in consequences. They do not learn that acceptable behavior requires self-discipline. They are confused because they believe that they can do whatever they want, and yet things do not go smoothly for them.

Discipline and control must be present in classrooms if learning is to occur as intended. Students *want* guidance and leadership. They are willing to accept guidance if it is not forced on them and if they believe they are being heard. This does not mean that they want to run the show.

Democratic Teachers

Ms. Tallers enters the room casually, greeting a few students near her. She asks the class to be seated and waits until she has everyone's attention. She asks for student input into certain matters of classroom routines and considers the suggestions carefully. She pauses twice and sends meaningful looks to a pair of students who are visiting in the back of the room.

Democratic teachers like Ms. Tallers are neither permissive nor autocratic. They provide firm guidance and leadership by establishing rules and consequences. They motivate students from within. They maintain order and, at the same time, allow students to participate in decision making. Democratic teachers teach that freedom is tied to responsibility. They allow students freedom to choose their own behavior. They also teach students that they must suffer the consequences if they choose to misbehave. Through this process, students learn to behave in ways that get them what they want.

Students who fail to develop self-discipline limit their choices. They choose inappropriate behavior because they do not understand that it always brings negative consequences. Freedom grows from discipline. If students understand that consequences follow behavior they are more free to choose behavior that will get them what they want. Discipline involves teaching students to establish inner controls that allow them to choose behavior compatible with their best interests. Teaching self-discipline eliminates the need for constant corrective actions by the teacher.

According to Dreikurs, the following conditions foster a democratic classroom:

1. Order.
2. Limits.
3. Firmness and kindness. Firmness from teachers shows they respect themselves. Kindness shows they respect others.
4. Student involvement in establishing and maintaining rules.
5. Leadership from the teacher.
6. Inviting cooperation—eliminating competition.
7. A sense of belonging to a group.
8. Freedom to explore, discover, and choose acceptable behavior through understanding the responsibilities and consequences associated with it.

MISTAKEN GOALS

Dreikurs makes three very strong points in his writings. First, students are social beings who want to belong. All of their actions reflect their attempts to be significant and gain acceptance. Second, students can choose to behave or misbehave. Their behavior is not outside their control. Putting these two beliefs together, Dreikurs makes his third point: Students choose to misbehave because they are under the mistaken belief that it will get them the recognition they seek. Dreikurs calls these beliefs mistaken goals.

All people want to belong, to have a place. They try all kinds of behavior to see if it gets them status and recognition. If they do not receive recognition through socially acceptable means they turn to mistaken goals, which produce antisocial behavior. Antisocial behavior reflects the mistaken belief that misbehavior is the only way to receive recognition.

Dreikurs identified four mistaken goals: *attention getting*, *power seeking*, *revenge seeking*, and *displaying inadequacy*. These goals identify the purposes of student misbehavior. They are usually sought in sequential order. If attention getting fails to gain recognition, the student will progress to power seeking. If that is not rewarded the student moves on to seeking revenge, and then to displaying inadequacy. Let's examine each of these mistaken goals more closely in the following paragraphs.

Attention Getting

When students discover that they are not getting the recognition they desire, they may resort to trying to get attention through misbehavior. These students are trying to seek proof of acceptance through what they can get others to give them, in this case, attention. They want the teacher to pay attention to them and provide them with extra services. They disrupt, ask special favors, continually need help with assignments, refuse to work unless the teacher hovers over them, or they ask irrelevant questions. Some good students can also make unusual bids for attention. They can function only as long as they have the teacher's approval. If that approval is not forthcoming, they may resort to less acceptable ways of getting attention.

Giving attention to misbehaving students does not improve their behavior; it reinforces it. Their need for attention increases. Furthermore, it causes them to be motivated by outside forces, rather than from within.

If attention-getting behavior does not provide students the recognition they seek, they will turn to the next mistaken goal—power.

Power Seeking

Power-seeking students feel that defying adults is the only way they can get what they want. Their mistaken belief is: If you don't let me do what I want, you don't approve of me. A need for power is expressed by arguing, contradicting, lying, having temper tantrums, and exhibiting hostility. If these students can get the teacher to fight with them they *win*, because they succeed in getting the teacher into a power struggle. Whether or not they actually get what they want does not matter. What does matter is that they upset the teacher. Should the teacher win the contest of wills, it only causes the student to believe more firmly that power is what matters in life. If students lose these power struggles, they move on to more severe misbehavior—getting revenge.

Revenge Seeking

Students have failed to gain status through getting attention or establishing power. Their mistaken goal now becomes: I can only feel significant if I have the power to hurt others. Hurting others makes up for being hurt.

Students who seek revenge set themselves up to be punished. They are vicious, cruel, and violent. When adults punish them, revenge-seeking students have renewed cause for action. The more trouble they cause for themselves, the more justified they feel. They consider it a victory to be disliked.

Underneath their bravado these individuals are deeply discouraged. Their behavior only elicits more hurt from others. They feel totally worthless and unlovable, and these feelings cause them to withdraw to the next mistaken goal—displaying inadequacy.

Displaying Inadequacy

At this level students feel themselves helpless and see themselves as total failures. There is no need to try anymore. They withdraw from any situation that can intensify their feeling of failure. They guard what little self-esteem they have left by removing it from social tests. Their mistaken belief is: If others believe I am inadequate they will leave me alone.

Students with this goal play stupid. They refuse to respond to motivation and passively refuse to participate in classroom activities. They do not interact with anyone. Dreikurs calls them "blobs." This mistaken goal is very serious and difficult for students and teachers to overcome.

All of the mistaken goals are based on the belief that they provide a way to achieve significance. Most mistaken goals are pursued only one at a time, but some students occasionally switch back and forth from one goal to another.

WHAT CAN TEACHERS DO?

The first thing teachers can do is identify the student's mistaken goal. The easiest way for teachers to do this is to note their own responses to the misbehavior. Their responses indicate what type of expectations the student has. If teachers feel:

- *Annoyed*, it indicates attention-getting behavior
- *Threatened*, it indicates power-seeking behavior
- *Hurt*, it indicates revenge
- *Powerless*, it indicates student displaying inadequacy

Another way to identify mistaken goals is to observe students' reactions to being corrected.

If students:	*Then their goal is:*
Stop the behavior and then repeat it	Getting attention
Refuse to stop, or increase the behavior	Power seeking
Become violent or hostile	Getting revenge
Refuse to cooperate, participate, or interact	Displaying inadequacy

After the teacher has identified the mistaken goals, the students should be confronted with an explanation of the mistaken goals together with a discussion of the faulty logic involved. By doing this in a friendly, nonthreatening way, teachers can usually get students to examine the purposes behind their behavior.

Dreikurs would have teachers ask students the following questions, in order, and observe reactions that might indicate a mistaken goal.

1. Could it be that you want me to pay attention to you?
2. Could it be that you want to prove that nobody can make you do anything?
3. Could it be that you want to hurt me or others?
4. Could it be that you want me to believe you are not capable?

These questions have three effects. They open up communication between teacher and student; they improve behavior because they remove the fun of provoking the teacher; and they take the initiative away from the student, allowing the teacher to implement actions to change behavior.

When teachers know the mistaken goals that are being aimed at, they can begin to take action that will defeat the student's purposes and initiate new, constructive behavior. Dreikurs recommends teachers take the following steps in each case of mistaken goals.

For Attention Getting

When teachers discover students seeking the mistaken goal of attention getting, they can either agree to go on giving attention, or they can refuse to grant attention or services by ignoring students when they are bidding for attention. Students who seek attention cannot tolerate being ignored. They would rather be punished, belittled, or humiliated, anything as long as they are getting someone to give them something. So, they create behavior that cannot be ignored by the teacher. Teachers who fall for this behavior nag, coax, scold, or otherwise reinforce the student's need for attention.

When teachers perceive that students are making undue bids for attention they should consistently and without fail ignore all such behavior. If they do so, the students will not get what they need from their behavior and will be forced to find new ways to gain recognition.

In addition to ignoring, teachers should strive to give attention to these students any time they are not demanding it. This encourages students to develop motivation from within instead of depending on attention from without.

Sometimes it is not feasible for teachers to ignore behavior that is disrupting the class. In such cases, teachers need to give attention in ways that are not rewarding to the student. The teacher may call the student's name and make eye contact without any comments. Or the teacher may describe the behavior without any trace of annoyance.

Example: "I see that you are not finishing your assignment."

One technique that has been partially effective is to privately confront the student with his goal and ask, "How many times do you think you will need my attention in the next hour?" The students will usually not know what to say. The teacher might then say, "If I give you attention 15 times, will that be enough?" This will sound like an exaggeration to the student. Then when the student misbehaves the teacher responds by saying, "Joel, number 1," "Joel, number 2," and so forth. The teacher does not comment on the behavior or scold, which would give Joel the attention he seeks, but simply lets him know that his behavior is being observed but not tolerated.

? Humiliation

By encouraging students to seek attention through useful behavior teachers inform students that they can receive recognition through good efforts and accomplishments. This helps students feel pride in themselves. Learning to function for self-satisfaction can be one of the most valuable lessons taught in school.

For Power Seeking

Most teachers react to power struggles by feeling threatened. They fight back, refusing to let students get the best of them. By fighting and winning struggles, teachers only cause students to become more rebellious and hostile and to think about getting revenge. Dreikurs believes that teachers do not have to fight with students nor give in. The best thing for them to do is not to get involved in power struggles in the first place. They should withdraw as an authority figure. The student cannot meet a goal of power if there is no one with whom to fight. Teachers may admit to the student and the class that they recognize the need for power. One way is to stop the entire class and have them wait for the disruptive behavior to cease, in which case the student is in conflict with peers and not the teacher.

Teachers can also redirect students' ambitions to be in charge by inviting them to participate in making decisions or by giving them positions of responsibility. A teacher might take a student aside and say, "The language during physical education is very unsportsmanlike. The others look up to you. Do you think you could help out by setting an example?" Or in the same situation the teacher might say, "I have a problem. It concerns the language I am hearing. What do you think I should do?" In this way, teachers admit that the student has power but refuse to be engaged in conflicts.

Teachers may also wish to confront the behavior openly. When a disruption begins they would say, "I cannot continue to teach when you are doing that. Can you think of a way in which you could do what you want and I could still teach?" If students cannot think of any ways, be prepared to suggest some alternatives.

By withdrawing as a power figure, teachers take fuel from a student's fire. Students cannot be involved in a power struggle with themselves. They will not receive status or recognition if they cannot get the best of the teacher. Teachers who withdraw thwart the purpose of power-seeking behavior.

For Revenge Seeking

The goal of revenge is closely related to the goal of power. Some students feel they should be allowed to do whatever they please and should consider anyone who tries to stop them as an enemy. These students are very difficult to deal with because they do not care about consequences. Consequences only give them justification for revenge.

It is difficult for teachers to care for students who are out to hurt them. These students feel the need to hurt others because they have been hurt themselves. What they need most is understanding and acceptance. Teachers can best provide this by calling on the class to support and encourage these students. Sometimes this is best accomplished by selecting a student with high esteem to befriend the troublemaker and help him or her develop constructive behavior. The teacher also may be able to set up situations that allow revengeful students to exhibit talents or strengths, helping to persuade these students that they can behave in ways that bring acceptance and status.

This is a very difficult thing to ask of a class. Students who seek revenge at first reject efforts made by others. Teachers must encourage their students and persuade them that their efforts will pay off. It is awful for any student to feel unliked by everyone. It takes persistence and patience on everyone's part to change such a situation.

For Displaying Inadequacy

Students who wish to be left alone usually think of themselves as thoroughly inadequate. They want their teacher to believe that they are too hopeless to deal with. Teachers often believe exactly that and promptly give up. After all, the students are not troublemakers—they are not disruptive or hostile. They are simply blobs. Students who adopt this goal usually do so for one of the following reasons:

1. They are overly ambitious. They cannot do as well as they think they should. If they cannot be the best, they will not put forth any effort at all.
2. They are overly competitive. They cannot do as well as others. They feel that they are not good enough. They withdraw from being compared.
3. They are under too much pressure. They cannot do as well as others want them to. They don't feel good enough as they are. They refuse to live up to anyone's expectations.

In each case, discouraged students feel like failures. They feel worthless and inadequate. They want to keep others from discovering exactly how useless they are.

Teachers must *never* give up on these students. They must always offer encouragement and support for even the smallest efforts. Encouragement is especially needed when the student is making mistakes. It is not the achievement but the effort that counts. Every attempt should be made by teachers and peers to make these students feel successful.

Teachers should also be very sensitive to their own reactions to these students. Any indication of defeat or frustration on the teacher's part reinforces the student's conviction of worthlessness and a desire to appear inadequate. One failure does not mean a student is a failure forever, and teachers must help encourage students to see this fact.

FOUR CASES OF MISTAKEN GOALS

Sally

Ms. Morton's class was doing independent seat work. Every few minutes Sally raised her hand to ask for some kind of direction: Should she number the sentences? Should she put her name on the paper? Was this answer right? Ms. Morton became very exasperated. Many times in the past she had had to explain things over and over to Sally. Finally she told Sally she would not help her anymore during seat work. She said she would explain the directions to the class once, and if Sally did not understand them she would have to wait and do the assignment at recess. Ms. Morton then ignored all Sally's requests for help. She did, however, immediately encourage Sally when she saw her working without assistance.

Sally's case is an example of attention-getting behavior. The best clue was the teacher's reaction—*annoyance*—to Sally's behavior. But Ms. Morton did the best thing in this instance. She ignored Sally's bids for attention while reinforcing her ability to work independently. She also established logical consequences for Sally's failure to work independently.

Jerry

Jerry and another student were scuffling near dangerous equipment in woodshop class. They knew this was against the rules and would result in their being removed temporarily from the class. Mr. Graves approached them and asked them to leave. Jerry refused. Mr. Graves was tempted to remove him physically. Instead, he walked to the front of the room and told everyone to turn off their machines and put their work down. He explained to the students that woodshop could not continue because Jerry was behaving in a dangerous way around equipment and refused to follow the class rule and leave the room. The class waited, not without directing looks at Jerry. Jerry soon chose to leave the shop.

Jerry's was an example of power-seeking behavior. Mr. Graves's first reaction was to feel his authority *threatened*. He was tempted to get into a power struggle with Jerry. However, he refused to be drawn into a fight. He freely admitted to the class that Jerry had the power to stop them from continuing. Jerry then had no one to struggle against. His power-seeking behavior was thwarted. Later, Mr. Graves asked Jerry to be a member of a group to review the rules for the class. That gave Jerry a position of authority that met his need for power in a constructive manner.

Julie

Julie was looking at a book that Miss Allen had brought in to read to the class. Cindy came over and grabbed it away, saying that she was supposed to get to see it first. Miss Allen gave the book back to Julie and scolded Cindy. When Miss Allen was straightening the room after school, she found the book with pages torn out and cover ripped. She felt certain that Cindy had destroyed the book, and was hurt and angered. Miss Allen had punished Cindy and Cindy had taken revenge. Her revenge hurt Miss Allen, which was what Cindy intended.

Miss Allen might have handled the situation better by suggesting that Julie and Cindy sit down and read the book together. Cindy would have felt accepted and included, rather than rejected.

Cathy

Mr. Redding gave the class an assignment to write a story. Everyone was soon busily writing, except for Cathy. Mr. Redding walked over to her and said, "Cathy, you can start by writing your name on your paper." Cathy did not pick up her pencil, but continued staring at her paper. Mr. Redding felt frustrated, but he did not feel like coaxing Cathy. He felt like saying, fine, if you don't want to work I won't waste my time on you. Instead he said, "Sometimes writers need time to think before they write. I know you'll start writing when you are ready."

Cathy wanted Mr. Redding to see her as inadequate. If she had wanted attention she would have responded to the teacher. Instead she acted as though he was not there, hoping he would go away. Mr. Redding did not give up as Cathy wished. He offered encouragement and let her know that he had faith in her ability to do the assignment.

ENCOURAGEMENT VERSUS PRAISE

Teachers have long used a variety of undesirable discipline techniques to deal with disruptive behavior. They have threatened, humiliated, and punished. They have waited for misbehavior to occur and then pounced. The results have been student resentment, rebellion, and hostility. Today's teachers need new approaches for effective classroom control, many of which are being explored. One of the most promising is *encouragement.* Dreikurs believes that encouragement is a crucial element in the prevention of problem behavior. Through encouragement teachers make learning seem worthwhile and help students develop positive self-concepts.

Encouragement consists of words or actions that convey teacher respect and belief in students' abilities. It tells students that they are accepted as they are. It recognizes efforts, not achievements. It gives students the courage to try, while accepting themselves as less than perfect. Teachers should be continually alert for opportunities to recognize effort, regardless of its results.

Encouragement facilitates feelings of being a contributing and participating member of a group. It helps students accept themselves as they are. It draws on motivation from within and allows them to become aware of their strengths.

Praise is different from encouragement. Praise is given when a task is done well. It promotes the idea that a product is worthless unless it receives praise. Students learn to receive praise from without and fail to learn to work for self-satisfaction. Praise encourages the attitude, "What am I going to get out of it?" Here are some examples showing the differences between praise and encouragement:

Praise	*Encouragement*
You are such a good girl for finishing your assignment.	I can tell that you have been working hard.
I am proud of you for behaving so well in the assembly.	Isn't it nice that we could all enjoy the assembly!
You play the guitar so well!	I can see that you really enjoy playing the guitar.

Dreikurs outlines the following pointers for teachers to use in encouraging students:

1. Always be positive; avoid negative comments.
2. Encourage students to strive for improvement, not perfection.
3. Encourage effort. Results don't matter so long as students are trying.
4. Emphasize strengths and minimize weaknesses.
5. Teach students to learn from mistakes. Emphasize that mistakes are not failures.
6. Stimulate motivation from within. Do not exert pressure from without.
7. Encourage independence.
8. Let students know that you have faith in their abilities.
9. Offer to help overcome obstacles.
10. Encourage students to help classmates who are having difficulties. This helps them appreciate their own strengths.
11. Send positive notes home, especially noting effort.
12. Show pride in students' work. Display the work and invite others to see it.
13. Be optimistic and enthusiastic—it is catching.
14. Try to set up situations that guarantee success for all.
15. Use encouraging remarks often, such as:
    You have improved!
    Can I help you?
    What did you learn from that mistake?
    I know you can.
    Keep trying!

> I know you can solve this, but if you think you need help...
> I understand how you feel, but I am sure you can handle it.

Dreikurs points out that there are also pitfalls in using encouragement. He cautions that teachers *should not*:

- Encourage competition or comparison with others.
- Point out how much better the student *could* be.
- Use "but" statements, such as "I'm pleased with your progress, but..."
- Use statements such as "It's about time."
- Give up on those who are not responding. Always encourage consistently and constantly.

LOGICAL CONSEQUENCES

No matter how encouraging teachers are, they will still encounter behavior problems. Dreikurs advises setting up "logical consequences" to help deter misbehavior and motivate appropriate behavior. Logical consequences are results that follow certain behaviors; they are arranged by the teacher.

Logical consequences must be differentiated from punishment. Punishment is action taken by the teacher to get back at misbehaving students and show them who is boss. Punishment breeds retaliation and gives students the feeling that they have the right to punish in return. Logical consequences on the other hand are not weapons used by the teacher. They teach students that all behavior produces a corresponding result: Good behavior brings rewards and unacceptable behavior brings unpleasant consequences. If a student throws paper on the floor, that student must pick it up. If a student fails to do work as assigned, that student must make up the work on his or her own time.

Logical consequences must be explained, understood, and agreed to by students. If they are sprung on students at the time of conflict, they will be considered punishment. When applying consequences, teachers should not act as self-appointed authorities. They should simply represent the order required by society and enforce the rules agreed to by the students.

Consequences are effective only when applied consistently. If teachers apply them while in a bad mood, or only to certain students, students will not learn that misbehavior *always* carries unpleasant consequences. They will misbehave and gamble when they can get away with it. Students must be convinced that consequences will be applied each and every time they choose to misbehave. They will have to consider carefully whether misbehaving is worth it. Sometimes it takes time to break old behavior habits, but teachers should never get discouraged and give up on implementing consequences.

Applying consequences allows students to make their own choices about how they will behave. They learn to rely on their own inner discipline to control their actions. They learn that poor choices invariably result in unpleasant consequences. It is nobody's fault but their own. Students also learn that the teacher respects their ability to make their own decisions.

Consequences should relate as closely as possible to the misbehavior, so students can see the connection between them. For example:

1. Students who damage school property would have to replace it.
2. Failure to complete an assignment would mean having to complete it after school.
3. Fighting at recess would result in no recess.
4. Disturbing others would result in isolation from the group.

Teachers should not show anger or triumph when applying consequences. They should simply say, "You chose to talk instead of doing math, so you must finish your math after school." When students choose to misbehave, they choose to suffer the consequences. Their action has nothing to do with the teacher's reaction.

DREIKURS' DOS AND DON'TS

Discipline involves ongoing teacher guidance to help students develop inner controls. It should not consist of limits imposed from the outside at times of stress and conflict. Rather, it should be consistent guidance that promotes a feeling of cooperation and team effort. To achieve this feeling, Dreikurs (1982) suggests that teachers do several things, among which are the following:

Teachers Should:
1. Give clear-cut directions for the actions expected of students. Wait until you have the attention of all class members before giving directions.
2. Try to establish a relationship with each individual, built on trust and mutual respect.
3. Use logical consequences instead of traditional punishment. The consequence must bear a direct relationship to the behavior and must be understood by students.
4. See behavior in its proper perspective. In this way, you will avoid making serious issues out of trivial incidents.

5. Let students assume greater responsibility for their own behavior and learning.
6. Treat students as your social equals.
7. Combine kindness and firmness. The student must always sense that you are a friend, but that you would not accept certain kinds of behavior.
8. At all times distinguish between the deed and the doer. This permits respect for the student, even when he or she does something wrong.
9. Set limits from the beginning, but work toward mutual understanding, a sense of responsibility, and consideration for others.
10. Mean what you say, but keep your demands simple, and see that they are carried out.
11. Close an incident quickly and revive good spirits. Let students know that mistakes are corrected, then forgotten.

Teachers Should Not:
1. Nag and scold, since this fortifies a student's mistaken concept of how to get attention.
2. Ask a student to promise anything. Most students will promise to change in order to get out of an uncomfortable situation. It is a sheer waste of time.
3. Find fault with students. It may hurt their self-esteem and discourage them.
4. Adopt double standards—one for yourself and another for the students.
5. Use threats as a method to discipline students. Although some students may become intimidated and conform for the moment, threats have no lasting value since they do not change students' basic attitudes.

COMMENTS ON DREIKURS' VIEWS

Of all the models presented so far, Dreikurs' views have the greatest potential for bringing about genuine attitudinal change among students, so that they ultimately behave better because they consider it the proper thing to do. Dreikurs continually refers to his approach as *democratic*, meaning that teachers and students together decide on rules and consequences, and that they take joint responsibility for maintaining a classroom climate conducive to learning.

Dreikurs would also have teachers spend considerable time talking with students about their actions, efforts, and results—about how they affect themselves and others. This puts teachers more strongly into a counseling role than is the case for other models, very effective if teachers possess such skills. Unfortunately, many do not, never having had such training.

For all its strengths, Dreikurs' system must be worked at over time for its valuable results to become evident. Moreover, it contains a possible defect that worries teachers of hard-to-manage classes—specifically, what do you do when students defy you? Dreikurs says to admit, before the class, that you cannot win a power struggle with misbehaving students. But he seems to suggest that the remainder of the class will side with the teacher and thus subtly direct the misbehaving student into compliance. Experienced teachers know, however, that defiant behavior is often strongly reinforced by other class members, and that it is sometimes contagious. They feel that such behavior must be stopped at once. Dreikurs does not say how that is to be done.

Despite that significant limitation, Dreikurs' emphasis on mutual respect, encouragement, student effort, and general responsibility are among the most powerful techniques for building desirable human character. Overall, Dreikurs' greatest contribution lies not in how immediately to suppress undesired behavior, but in how to build, in students, an inner sense of responsibility and respect for others.

Application Exercises

CASE #1. KRIS WILL NOT WORK:

Kris, a student in Mr. Jake's class, is quite docile. She socializes little with other students and never disrupts the class. But despite Mr. Jake's best efforts, Kris will not do her work. She rarely completes an assignment. She is simply there, like a bump on a log, putting forth no effort.

How would Dreikurs deal with Kris? Dreikurs would suggest that Mr. Jake follow these steps as a means of improving Kris's behavior:

1. Identify Kris's mistaken goal. (Mr. Jake can do this by checking his own reaction to Kris's lethargy and by noting the reactions of other students when he attempts to correct her.)
2. If Kris's mistaken goal is attention-getting, ignore her.
3. If Kris's mistaken goal is power-seeking, admit that Kris has power. "I can't make you do your work. What do you think I should do?"
4. If Kris's goal is revenge, ask other members of the class to be especially encouraging to her.
5. If Kris's goal is inadequacy, encourage her frequently and give her continual support.

6. Confront Kris with her mistaken goal and draw her into a discussion about the goal and her behavior.

CASE #2. TOM IS HOSTILE AND DEFIANT:

Tom has appeared to be in his usual foul mood ever since arriving in class. He gets up and on his way to sharpen his pencil he bumps into Frank. Frank complains. Tom tells him loudly to shut up. Miss Baines, the teacher, says "Tom, go back to your seat." Tom wheels around, swears loudly and says heatedly "I'll go when I'm damned good and ready!"

How would Dreikurs suggest that Miss Baines deal with Tom?

ACTIVITIES:

For each of the following cases, (a) identify the student's mistaken goal and (b) explain how Dreikurs would have the teacher deal with it.

1. Joey habitually plays with treasured objects in his desk when he should be listening. This causes his teacher to stop instruction frequently and remind him to listen. He usually complies for a few minutes.
2. Robin seems to have made it her life's goal to taunt and belittle her classmates. If they notify the teacher about her behavior, she harasses them on the playground.
3. Maria sits in the back of the classroom. She stares at her desk. She has never turned in an assignment. She does not speak when spoken to.
4. Susan likes to enter the classroom five minutes late, making enough noise to distract the class. When asked to explain her tardiness she accuses the teacher of picking on her.

REFERENCES

Dreikurs, R. (1968). *Psychology in the classroom* (2nd ed). New York: Harper and Row.

Dreikurs, R., & Cassel, P. (1972). *Discipline without tears*. New York: Hawthorn.

Dreikurs, R., Grunwald, B., & Pepper, F. (1982). *Maintaining sanity in the classroom*. New York: Harper and Row.

CHAPTER 6

The Jones Model:

Body Language, Incentive Systems, and Providing Efficient Help

JONES BIOGRAPHICAL SKETCH

Frederic H. Jones, a psychologist, is director of the Classroom Management Training Program, headquartered in Santa Cruz, California, where
he is developing and promoting procedures for improving teacher effectiveness, especially in the areas of student motivation and behavior management. His programs provide staff development for many school districts.
The procedures he advocates initially grew out of research and development in classroom practices, conducted while he was on the faculties of the
U.C.L.A. Medical Center and the University of Rochester School of
Medicine and Dentistry. His work is received enthusiastically by teachers,
who recognize in it refinements of practices with which they are already
familiar but have not seen organized into a systematic approach. Unlike
the other major authorities, Jones only recently published a book on his
management system, relying earlier on his "pyramid" training system, in
which teachers are trained to train other teachers with whom they work.
Jones's book, *Positive Classroom Discipline*, was published in 1987.

JONES'S MAIN FOCUS

The main focus of Jones's model of discipline is on helping students support
their own self control (Jones, 1979). Toward that end he emphasizes effective use of body language, describes how to provide incentives that motivate desired behavior, and details procedures for providing effective and
efficient help to students during independent work time.

Jones's Key Ideas

1. Teachers in typical classrooms lose approximately 50% of their
   instructional time because students are off task or otherwise disturbing the teacher or other class members.
2. Practically all of this lost time results from two kinds of student
   misbehavior—talking without permission (80%) and general
   goofing off, including making noises, daydreaming, or getting out
   of one's seat without permission.
3. Most of this lost teaching time can be salvaged if teachers systematically employ three kinds of techniques that strongly assist discipline: (1) effective body language; (2) incentive systems; and
   (3) efficient individual help.
4. Good classroom discipline results mainly from the first technique—
   effective body language, which includes posture, eye contact, facial
   expression, signals, gestures, and physical proximity.

5. Incentive systems, which motivate students to remain on task, complete work, and behave properly, also contribute strongly to good discipline.

6. When teachers are able to provide individual help to students quickly and effectively, the students behave better and complete more work.

JONES'S CONCLUSIONS ABOUT MISBEHAVIOR AND TIME LOSS

During the 1970s Frederic Jones and his associates conducted thousands of hours of carefully controlled observations in hundreds of elementary and secondary classrooms in various parts of the country. Their concern lay in effective methods of classroom management, especially in how teachers attempted to keep students working on task, how they provided individual help when needed, and how they dealt with misbehavior.

Their observations led them to several important conclusions. Principal among them was that classroom discipline problems are generally quite different from the way they are depicted in the media and perceived by the public. Even though many of the classrooms Jones studied were located in inner-city schools and alternative schools for students with behavior problems, Jones found no terrorism, no bullying attacks on teachers, and very little hostile defiance—the kinds of behavior that teachers fear and that many people believe exist in the schools. Instead, they found what Jones called "massive time wasting," which was comprised almost entirely of students talking, goofing off, and moving about the room without permission. Jones found that in well-managed classrooms, one of those behaviors occurred about every two minutes. In loud, unruly classes the disruptions averaged about 2.5 per minute. In attempting to deal with those misbehaviors, teachers lost almost 50% of the time available for teaching and learning.

The teachers, Jones found, typically felt frustrated in their efforts to manage classrooms. Many of them expressed bitterness that they had never received training in how to deal effectively with misbehavior. New teachers expected that they would quickly learn to maintain order in their classrooms, but most were only partially successful, and many soon resorted to hostility and punitive measures or else threw up their hands in resignation. The overall results were loss of teaching and learning time, lowered levels of student learning, and high levels of teacher frustration and stress.

Jones concluded that teachers were correct in their contentions that they had not received training in behavior management, and further that many, if not most, were unable to develop needed skills while working on the job. Jones decided to carefully observe and document the methods used by those few teachers who were notably successful with discipline. From those observations he identified specific clusters of skills that served both to forestall misbehavior and to deal with it quickly when it did occur. Three such skill clusters emerged—one having to do with *body language*, a second having to do with motivation through the use of *incentive systems*, and a third having to do with *providing help efficiently* to individual students. Jones now instructs teachers and administrators in the use of these skill clusters through his Classroom Management Training Program.

Skill Cluster #1: Body Language

Jones maintains that good discipline depends mostly—90% he says—on effective body language. Therefore, his training program concentrates on helping teachers learn to use their physical mannerisms to set and enforce behavior limits. (These limits are also specified in class rules.) This body language involves eye contact, physical proximity, body carriage, facial expression, and gestures. At its most effective level, it communicates that the teacher is calmly in control, knows what is going on, and means business. The following paragraphs present Jones's views on the various aspects of body language.

Eye Contact. Jacob has stopped paying attention. Miss Remy pauses. The sudden change in her lesson causes Jacob to look at Miss Remy, to find that she is looking directly at his eyes. He straightens up and waits attentively.

Few physical acts are more effective than eye contact for conveying the impression of being in control. Skilled teachers allow their eyes to sweep the room continually, and as they do so they pause directly on the eyes of individual students. Locking eyes makes many people uncomfortable, teachers and students alike, and students often avert their eyes when teachers look directly at them. The effect is not lost, however, for the students realize that the teacher, in looking directly at them, takes continual note of their behavior, both good and bad.

Making eye contact does not seem to be a natural behavior for most beginning teachers and therefore must be practiced before it can be used effectively. Inexperienced teachers tend to look over students' heads, between them, or dart their eyes rapidly without locking onto individuals. Sometimes while teaching, they stare more or less directly ahead, failing to monitor students who are located at the backs and sides of the group, or they find comfort in looking only at the faces of two or three well-behaved, actively responding students, oblivious to others not so attuned to the lesson.

These tendencies carry over into subsequent years, so it is common to encounter experienced teachers who do not use eye contact effectively. With practice, however, they can learn to focus their eyes directly on the face of each individual student. This in itself sends a message that the teacher is aware and in control. It further serves to inhibit students who are on the verge of misbehaving, and it provides an opportunity to send facial expressions of approval or disapproval.

Physical Proximity. Jacob has stopped working on his assignment and begun talking to Jerry. Suddenly he sees the shadow of Miss Remy at his side. He immediately gets back to work, without anything being said.

In his classroom observations, Jones noted that most misbehavior occurred some distance away from the teacher. Students near the teacher rarely misbehaved. This phenomenon has long been recognized by experienced teachers, who have learned to move nearer to students who are prone to misbehave, or to seat such students near them.

Jones also noted that teachers who used physical proximity did not need to say anything to the offending students to get them to behave. He therefore concluded that verbalization was not needed, that in fact it sometimes weakened the effect, due possibly to defensive reactions engendered in students when reprimanded verbally. Teachers who need to deal with minor misbehavior are instructed to move near the offending student, establish brief eye contact, and say nothing. The student will usually return immediately to proper behavior.

To use physical proximity effectively, the teacher must be able to step quickly alongside the appropriate student. This is difficult in traditionally arranged classrooms because students are seated in long rows of desks or clusters of tables spread out over most of the floor space. Jones would have teachers seat students in shallow semicircles, no more than three rows deep, with walk space interspersed. The teacher can then operate from within the arc of the semicircle, obtain easy eye contact with students, and move quickly to the side of any student. This arrangement also allows teachers to provide individual help much more quickly, as will be discussed later in the chapter.

Body Carriage. Jones says that body posture and carriage can be quite effective in communicating authority. Students quickly read such body language and are able to tell whether the teacher is ill, tired, disinterested, or intimidated. Good posture and confident carriage suggest strong leadership; a drooping posture and lethargic movements suggest resignation or fearfulness. Effective teachers even when tired or troubled tend to hold themselves erect and move with a measure of vigor. One should note here that on those infrequent occasions when the teacher is feeling ill, it is a good idea to inform the students and ask for their assistance and tolerance.

Students usually behave with unexpected consideration at such times, although not when the strategy is used insincerely or too frequently.

Facial Expression. Like carriage, facial expression communicates much to students. It can show enthusiasm, seriousness, enjoyment, and appreciation, all of which tend to encourage good behavior; or it can reveal boredom, annoyance, and resignation, which may tend to encourage misbehavior. Perhaps more than anything else, facial expression, through winks, smiles, and contortions, can demonstrate a sense of humor, the trait that students say they like most in teachers.

The face can be put to good use in sending other types of nonverbal signals. Eye contact has been discussed as a prime example. Very slight shakes of the head can stop much misbehavior before it gets under way. Frowns show unmistakable disapproval. A firmed lip line and flashing eyes can indicate powerfully that the limits have been reached. These facial expressions are used instead of words whenever possible. They are as effective as words in showing approval, and for control and disapproval they have the advantage over verbal rebuffs in that they seldom belittle, sting, antagonize, or provoke counterattacks from students.

Gestures. Experienced teachers employ a variety of hand signals that they use to encourage and discourage behavior and to maintain student attention. Examples include palm out (*stop*), palm up flexing fingers (*continue*), finger to lips (*quiet*), finger snap (*attention*), and thumbs up (*approval*). These gestures communicate effectively, do not interfere with necessary instructional verbalization, and have other advantages over verbal reprimands that have already been discussed.

A Case Of Body Language In Use. The following is an example of body language put to use as suggested by Jones:

1. Sam and Jim are talking and laughing while Mr. Sanchez is explaining the process used to divide fractions. Mr. Sanchez makes eye contact with them, pauses momentarily, and then continues with his explanation. Sam and Jim probably stop talking when Mr. Sanchez looks at them and pauses. But if they continue . . .
2. Mr. Sanchez again pauses, makes eye contact, and shakes his head slightly but emphatically. He may give a fleeting palm-out signal. Sam and Jim probably stop talking when he sends these signals. But if they continue . . .
3. Mr. Sanchez moves calmly and stands beside Sam and Jim. He asks the class, "Who thinks they can go to the board and show us how to divide five-eights by one-eighth? Tell us what to do, step by step."

Sam and Jim will almost certainly stop talking now. But if they continue...

4. Mr. Sanchez makes eye contact with them and calmly says, "Jim, Sam, I want you to stop talking right now."

If for any reason they defy Mr. Sanchez' direct order, Mr. Sanchez stops the lesson long enough to separate the boys, or seat them in opposite corners of the room, or as a last resort call the office to inform that they are being sent for detention. In any of these cases, a follow-up conference will be necessary with the boys, and if the defiance continues, it will need to dealt with by the principal, vice-principal, counselor, and/or the boys' parents.

Note that in all cases except the most severe, Mr. Sanchez used only body language. There was no verbal confrontation and only the slightest slowdowns in the lesson. Instruction continued, students were kept on task, and teaching-learning time was preserved.

Skill Cluster #2: Incentive Systems

Mr. Sharpe tells his class that if all of them complete their work in 45 minutes or less they can have the last 10 minutes of class time to talk quietly with a friend. Mr. Dulle tells his class that if they promise to work very hard later on, he will allow them to begin the period by discussing their work with a friend. Which teacher is likely to get the best work from his students?

This question has to do with the use of incentives. An incentive is something outside of the individual that prompts the individual to act. It is something that is promised as a consequence for desired behavior, but is held in abeyance, to occur or be provided later. It might be popcorn, a preferred activity, an unspecified surprise, and so forth. It is an effective incentive if students will behave as desired in order to obtain it later.

Jones gives incentives a prominent place in his classroom management program, as a means of motivating students. He found that some of the most effective teachers used incentives systematically, but that most teachers used them ineffectively or not at all. The ineffective teachers typically made use of marks, stars, having work displayed, being dismissed first, and so forth. The problem with such incentives is that they go only to the top achievers; the less able students, once out of contention for the prize, have nothing left for which to work. Moreover, for many students, receiving a badge or being first in line does not compete strongly with the joys of talking or daydreaming.

What, then, are characteristics of effective incentives and their use? Jones implies that teachers should emphasize genuineness, "Grandma's rule," educational value, and ease of implementation. Let us examine these suggestions further.

Genuine Incentives. There is a wide difference between what many teachers *hope* will be incentives (e.g., Let's all work in such a way that we will later be proud of what we do.) and what are genuine incentives from the student's point of view (e.g., If you complete your work on time you can have five minutes of free time to talk with your friends.) This point may seem obvious, but it is often overlooked. Teachers may say, "The first person to complete a perfect paper will receive two bonus points." This works to motivate a handful of students, but most know they have little chance to win so they barely try. Or they may say, "If you really try, you can be the best class I have ever had." This usually sounds better to the teacher than to the students. Although the students might like to think of themselves as the best, that thought will not be strong enough to keep them hard at work.

What, then, are some genuine incentives that can be used in the classroom? Generally, students respond well to the anticipation of preferred activities such as art, viewing a film, or having free time to pursue personal interests or to talk with friends. Such group activities are genuine incentives in that almost all students desire them sufficiently to make extra effort to obtain them. Many teachers use tangible objects, awards, and certificates as incentives. These are less desirable because they may be costly or difficult to dispense and they have little educational value.

Grandma's Rule. Grandma's rule goes like this: First eat your dinner and then you can have your dessert. Applied to the classroom, this rule requires that students first do what they are supposed to do, and then for a while they can do what they want to do. The incentive is the end product of the proposition. In order to obtain it, students must complete designated work while behaving acceptably.

Just as children (and many adults) will ask to have their dessert first, promising to eat all their dinner afterward, students will ask to have their incentive first, pledging on their honor to work feverishly afterward. As we all know, even the best intentions are hard to fulfill once the reason for doing so is gone. Thus, teachers who wish to use effective incentive systems must, despite student urging, delay the rewards until last and make the reward contingent on the students doing required work acceptably. In other words, "If they don't eat their beans and cabbage, they don't get their pudding."

Educational Value. To the extent feasible, every class period should be devoted to activities that have educational value. Work that only keeps students occupied, but teaches them little, can seldom be justified. This principle holds for incentive systems. While few educators would be such Scrooges that they would never allow a moment of innocent frivolity, the opposite extreme of throwing daily or weekly classroom parties as incentives for work and behavior is difficult to condone from an educational standpoint. What then should one do?

There are many educationally valuable activities that students enjoy greatly, both individually and in groups. One of the best for individuals is "free time," in which students may read, work on assignments, do art work, plan with other students, or pursue personal interests. Despite the word "free," students are not left to do just anything, nor do they proceed without rules of guidance. The freedom is that of choosing from a variety of approved activities.

For the total group, activities can be chosen by vote, and all students engage in the same activity during the time allotted. Elementary school students often select physical education, art, music, drama, or construction activities. Frequently, they want the teacher to read to them from a favorite book. Secondary students often choose to watch a film, hold class discussions on special topics, watch demonstrations and performances by class members, or work together on such projects as producing a class magazine.

Group Concern. As mentioned earlier, many classroom incentive systems in normal practice contain a fatal flaw. That flaw is that only a few students —the faster working, higher achieving—have a genuine opportunity to earn the incentive. Most of the others make only perfunctory effort, having learned that they have little chance of success.

Jones teaches a way around this flaw, one that involves every class member and yet remains simple to administer. His plan hinges on causing every student to have a stake in earning the incentive for the entire class. This motivates all students to keep on task, behave well, and complete assigned work. Here is how it works.

The teacher sets aside a period of time in which students can engage in a preferred activity. In keeping with Grandma's rule, this time period must come after a significant amount of work time devoted to the standard curriculum. It can be at the end of the school day for self-contained classes, perhaps 15 to 20 minutes. For departmentalized classes, the time can be set aside at the end of the week, perhaps 30 minutes on Friday. The students can decide on the activity for their "dessert" time, and to earn it they have only to work and behave as expected.

The teacher manages the system by using a stopwatch, preferably a large one with hands that the class can see. When any student begins to misbehave the teacher simply lifts the stopwatch and clicks it on. Every second that ticks off the watch is time deducted from the time originally available for the incentive. The teacher must be dispassionately firm in applying this technique. A burst of perfect behavior cannot be allowed to erase previous misbehavior, since that tells students it is all right to misbehave for a while before settling down. The teacher also must not be talked into canceling time lost on the promise of better behavior in the future. The students know the rules of the game from the beginning, and they know that they can choose through their behavior whether and to what extent they will earn the incentive time.

Teachers often think it unfair to penalize the entire class, through loss of time, for the sins of a few or even a single class member. In practice, this is rarely a problem because the class is made to understand that this is a group not an individual effort. The group is rewarded together and punished together regardless of who might transgress. A strength in this approach is that it brings to bear strong peer pressure against misbehavior. Ordinarily a misbehaving student obtains reinforcement from the group in the form of attention, laughter, or admiration. With the stopwatch system the opposite is true. The class is likely to discourage individual misbehavior because it takes away something the class members want.

Ease Of Implementation. Unlike other incentive systems, that advocated by Jones accomplishes two important ends simultaneously: first, it is effective for all students because all are brought into the picture; second, it is easy to implement. Teachers need do only four things:

1. Establish and explain the system.
2. Allow the class to vote from time to time on which teacher-approved activities they wish to enjoy during incentive time.
3. Obtain a stopwatch and use it conscientiously.
4. Be prepared when necessary to conduct the class in low-preference activities for the amount of time that students might have lost from their preferred activity time allotment.

When It Does Not Work. If an incentive system loses effectiveness, it is likely to be for one of the following reasons.

1. The preferred activities might have grown stale. This is cured by allowing the class to discuss the matter and decide on new preferences.
2. The class may temporarily be overly excited by unsettling occurrences such as unusual weather, a holiday, special events at school,

or an accident. In such cases the teacher may suspend the incentive program for a time, with explanation and discussion.

3. Individual students may occasionally lose self-control or decide to defy the teacher. In this case, the offending student should be isolated in the room or removed to the office. The teacher can establish a policy wherein the class will not be penalized for the actions of individual students that result in isolation or removal from the room.

Skill Cluster #3: Providing Efficient Help

One of the most interesting, important, and useful findings in Jones's research has to do with the way teachers provide individual help to students who are "stuck" during seat work. Suppose that a math lesson is in progress. The teacher introduces the topic, explains the algorithm on the chalkboard, asks a couple of questions to determine whether the students are understanding, and then assigns 10 problems from the textbook to be done by students at their desks. Very soon a hand is raised to signal that a student is stuck and needs help. If only three of four hands are raised during work time, the teacher has no problem. But if 20 students fill the air with waving arms, most of them will sit for several minutes doing nothing while awaiting attention from the teacher. For each student needing help this time is pure waste and an encouragement to misbehave.

Jones asked teachers how much time they thought they spent on the average when providing help to each student who signaled. The teachers felt that they spent from one to two minutes with each student, but when Jones's researchers timed the episodes they found that teachers actually spent around four minutes with each student. This consumed much time and made it impossible for the teacher to attend to more than a few students during work time. Even if the amount of time spent was only one minute per contact, some students would waste several minutes while waiting.

Jones noted another phenomenon that compounded the problem. He described it as a "dependency syndrome" wherein some students felt so uncomfortable doing independent work that they routinely raised their hands for teacher help even when they did not need it. To have the teacher unfailingly come to their side and give personal attention proved rewarding indeed, and that reinforcement further strengthened the dependency.

From these observations, Jones described independent seat work as having four inherent problems: (1) insufficient time for teachers to answer all requests for help; (2) wasted student time; (3) high potential for misbehavior; and (4) the perpetuation of dependency. Consequently, he gave this matter high priority in his classroom management training program.

Jones determined that all four problems could be solved through teaching teachers how to give help more efficiently. He would have this be accomplished in three steps:

- *Step one*: Organize the classroom seating so that students are within easy reach of the teacher. The shallow concentric semicircles previously described are suggested. Otherwise the teacher uses too much time and energy dashing from one end of the room to the other.
- *Step two*: Use graphic reminders, such as models or charts, that provide clear examples and instructions. These might show steps in algorithms, proper form for business letters, or simply written directions for the lesson. These reminders are posted and can be consulted by students before they call for teacher help.
- *Step three*: This step is one in which Jones places great stock. It involves learning how to cut to a bare minimum the time used to give individual help. To see how it is done, consider that teachers normally give help in the form of a questioning tutorial as follows:
  "What's the problem?"
  "All right, what did we say was the first thing to do?" (Waits; repeats question.)
  "No, that was the second. You are forgetting the first step. What was it? Think again." (Waits until student finally makes a guess.)
  "No, let me help you with another example. Suppose . . ."

Often in this helping mode the teacher virtually reteaches the concept or process to each student who requests help. That is how four minutes can be unexpectedly spent in each interaction. If help is to be provided more quickly, this questioning method must be reconsidered. Jones trains teachers to give help in a very different way, and *he insists that it be done in 20 seconds or less* for each student. Here is what the teacher should do when arriving beside the student:

1. Quickly find anything that the student has done correctly and mention it favorably. ("Your work is very neat" or "Good job up to here.")
2. Give a straightforward hint or suggestion that will get the student going. ("Follow step 2 on the chart" or "Regroup here.")
3. Leave immediately.

Help provided in this way solves the major problems that Jones identified. Teachers have time to attend to every student who needs help. Students spend little wasted time waiting for the teacher. Misbehavior is much less likely to occur. The dependency syndrome is broken, especially if the teacher gives attention to students who try to complete their work without calling for assistance. Rapid circulation by the teacher also permits better monitoring of work being done by students who do not raise their hands. When errors are noted in their work the teacher can provide the same kind of help as that given to the others.

JONES'S REMINDERS FOR TEACHERS

The three skill clusters described in this chapter—body language, incentive systems, and efficient help—comprise the core of Jones's system of discipline. Reminders for teachers were presented in a report by Rardin (1978):

- Catch misbehavior early and deal with it immediately.
- Use body language instead of words. Show you mean business through your posture, eye contact, facial expression, and gestures.
- Use physical proximity in dealing with misbehaving or defiant students.
- Use group incentive systems, (following Grandma's rule), to motivate work and good behavior.
- Provide individual help efficiently; aim for 10-second interactions.
- Do not use threats; establish rules and attend to misbehavior.

COMMENTS ON JONES'S MODEL

More than any of the other models, Jones has isolated behaviors seen in teachers who are often called "naturals" in working with students. That is why teachers' heads nod in agreement with his suggestions; they recognize the behaviors and the settings within which they occur. Jones has also found that most of those behaviors are teachable, although many teachers never learn them well within the pressures of day-to-day teaching. Through specific training episodes, most teachers can acquire the behaviors that typically characterize only the most effective.

But it is unrealistic to think that teachers can read Jones's work and then walk into the classroom the next day transformed. The acts he describes must be practiced repeatedly. Fortunately, teachers do not have to go to expensive, time-consuming training seminars to learn them. They can, instead, assess their own classroom behavior in light of Jones's suggestions and isolate certain behaviors they would like to improve. Then they can take the new learnings into the classroom one by one. That is one of the nice things about Jones's suggestions—they do not have to be taken as a full-blown total system into the classroom, but can instead be practiced, perfected, and added incrementally.

Application Exercises

CASE #1. KRIS WILL NOT WORK:

Kris, a student in Mr. Jake's class, is quite docile. She socializes little with other students and never disrupts the class. However, Mr. Jake cannot get Kris to do any work. She rarely completes an assignment. She is simply there, like a bump on a log, putting forth no effort at all.

How would Jones deal with Kris? Jones would suggest that Mr. Jake take the following steps to improve Kris's behavior.

1. Make frequent eye contact with her. Even when she looks down, he should make sure to look directly at her. She will be aware of it and it may make her uncomfortable enough that she will begin work.
2. Move close to Kris. Stand beside her while presenting the lesson.
3. Use encouraging facial expressions and hand signals every time eye contact can be made.
4. Give Kris frequent help during seat work. Check on her progress several times during the lesson; give specific suggestions; and move quickly on.
5. Set up a personal incentive system with Kris—a certain amount of work earns something that Kris values.
6. Set up a system in which Kris, by working, can earn rewards for the entire class. This brings added peer support to Kris.

CASE #2. TOM IS HOSTILE AND DEFIANT:

Tom has appeared to be in his usual foul mood ever since arriving in class. He gets up and on his way to sharpen his pencil he bumps into Frank. Frank complains. Tom tells him loudly to shut up. Miss Baines, the teacher, says "Tom, go back to your seat." Tom wheels around, swears loudly and says heatedly "I'll go when I'm damned good and ready!"

How would Jones suggest that Miss Baines deal with Tom?

ACTIVITIES:

For each of the following scenarios: (a) Identify the problem that underlies the undesired behavior and (b) Describe how Jones would have the teacher deal with it.

1. Mr. Anton tries to help all of his students during independent work time but finds himself unable to get around to all who have their hands raised.
2. Ms. Sevier wants to show trust for her class. She accepts their promise to work hard if they can first listen to a few favorite recorded

songs. After listening to the songs, the students talk so much that they fail to get their work done.

3. Mr. Gregory wears himself out every day dealing ceaselessly with three class clowns who disrupt his lessons. The other students always laugh at the clowns' antics.

REFERENCES

Jones, F. (1979). The gentle art of classroom discipline. *National Elementary Principal, 58,* 26–32.

Jones, F. (1987). *Positive Classroom Discipline.* New York: McGraw-Hill.

Rardin, R. (1978, September). Classroom management made easy. *Virginia Journal of Education,* 14–17.

CHAPTER 7

The Canter Model:

Assertively Taking Charge

CANTER BIOGRAPHICAL SKETCH

Lee Canter, trained as a specialist in child guidance, is director of Canter and Associates, a California-based organization that provides training in assertive discipline to parents and educators. Marlene Canter, his wife, has collaborated in much of the work. She has been a teacher of the learning disabled in various school districts in California. Canter's research into the behaviors of highly successful teachers led to the formulation of discipline system called "assertive discipline," which offers a means for interacting with students in a calm yet forceful manner. Assertive discipline has been widely accepted in schools across the nation. Canter and Associates, with a continuing heavy schedule of training workshops, have brought assertive discipline to hundreds of thousands of teachers and administrators nationwide.

CANTER'S MAIN FOCUS

The main focus of Canter's model is on assertively insisting on proper behavior from students, with well-organized procedures for following through when they do not. It provides a very strong system of corrective discipline.

Canter's Key Ideas

The following list presents the key ideas that form the core of assertive discipline, providing a summary of the assertive discipline model. These ideas are explained in greater detail in subsequent sections of this chapter.

1. Teachers should insist on decent, responsible behavior from their students. Students need this type of behavior, parents want it, the community at large expects it, and the educational process is ineffective without it.
2. Teacher failure, for all practical purposes, is synonymous with failure to maintain adequate classroom discipline.
3. Many teachers labor under false assumptions about discipline, believing that firm control is stifling and inhumane. To the contrary, firm control maintained correctly is humane and liberating.
4. Teachers have basic educational rights in their classrooms including:
   a. The right to establish optimal learning environments.
   b. The right to request and expect appropriate behavior.
   c. The right to receive help from administrators and parents when it is needed.

5. Students have basic rights in the classroom, too, including:
   a. The right to have teachers who help limit inappropriate, self-destructing behavior.
   b. The right to choose how to behave, with full understanding of the consequences that automatically follow their choices.
6. These needs, rights, and conditions are best met through assertive discipline, in which the teacher clearly communicates expectations to students and consistently follows up with appropriate actions but never violates the best interests of the students.
7. Assertive discipline consists of the following elements, to be followed consistently by teachers:
   a. Identifying expectations clearly.
   b. Willingness to say "I like that," and "I don't like that."
   c. Persistence in stating expectations and feelings.
   d. Use of firm tone of voice.
   e. Maintenance of eye contact.
   f. Use of nonverbal gestures in support of verbal statements.
   g. Use of hints, questions, and I-messages rather than demands for requesting appropriate behavior.
   h. Follow-through with promises (reasonable consequences, previously established) rather than with threats.
   i. Assertiveness in confrontations with students, including using statements of expectations, indicating consequences that will occur, and noting why action is necessary.
8. To become more assertive in discipline, teachers should do the following:
   a. Practice assertive response styles.
   b. Set clear limits and consequences.
   c. Follow through consistently.
   d. Make specific assertive discipline plans and rehearse them mentally.
   e. Write things down; do not trust the memory.
   f. Practice the broken record technique for repeating expectations.
   g. Ask school principals and parents for support in the efforts to help students.

THE NEED FOR ASSERTIVE DISCIPLINE

Discipline is a matter of great concern in schools; it remains so year after year. For teachers it is the overwhelming cause of failure, burn-out, and resignation. Parents and the community single it out as greatly in need of correction. Discipline has become a more serious problem over the last few decades, possibly as a result of declines in society's respect for authority and parents' requiring that their children behave acceptably in school. But schools and teachers deserve part of the blame, too. Societal conditions may make discipline more difficult, but mistaken ideas about discipline cause educators to be hesitant about controlling behavior.

Mistaken Ideas About Discipline

Mistaken ideas about discipline that are widely held by educators include:

1. Good teachers can handle discipline problems on their own without any help.
2. Firm discipline causes psychological trauma to students.
3. Discipline problems disappear when students are given activities that meet their needs.
4. Misbehavior results from deep-seated causes that are beyond the influence of the teacher.

Correct Ideas About Discipline

The mistaken ideas about discipline must be replaced by the following correct ideas, if discipline is to be effectively maintained:

1. We all need discipline for psychological security.
2. We all need discipline as a suppressant to acts that we would not be proud of later.
3. We all need discipline as a liberating influence that allows us to build and expand our best traits and abilities.
4. Discipline is necessary to maintain an effective and efficient learning environment.

THE BASIS OF ASSERTIVE DISCIPLINE

Canter maintains that an assertive teacher is one who *clearly and firmly communicates needs and requirements to students, follows those words with appropriate actions, responds to students in ways that maximize compliance, but in no way violates the best interests of the students.*

He says repeatedly that the basis of this assertive posture is *caring about oneself* to the point of not allowing students to take advantage and *caring about students* to the point of not allowing them to behave in ways that are damaging to themselves (Canter, 1978). This caring is shown by teachers who are positive, firm, and consistent, not wishy-washy, hostile, abusive, or threatening—negative behaviors that are certain to fail.

A climate of care and support rises up from what Canter calls "basic teacher rights" in working with students:

1. The right to establish optimal learning environments for students, consistent with the teacher's strengths and limitations.
2. The right to expect behavior from students that contributes to their optimal growth, while also meeting the special needs of the teacher.
3. The right to ask and receive help and backing from administrators and parents.

When these basic rights of teachers are met, they have the potential for providing a climate of positive support and care. But for that potential to be realized, more is needed. As you might imagine, that additional need is training in assertive discipline.

FIVE STEPS TO ASSERTIVE DISCIPLINE

Canter emphasizes that teachers can easily incorporate the basics of assertive discipline into their own teaching styles. A series of five steps is implied for this implementation, which appear to be: (1) recognizing and removing roadblocks to assertive discipline; (2) practicing the use of assertive response styles; (3) learning to set limits; (4) learning to follow through on limits; and (5) implementing a system of positive assertions. The five steps are explained and discussed in the paragraphs that follow.

Step 1. Recognizing and Removing Roadblocks to Assertive Discipline

All teachers have within themselves the potential for expressing their educational needs to students and for obtaining student compliance with those needs. Most teachers have difficulty, however, with both the expression and compliance, due to a group of "roadblocks" that hinder teachers' efforts to be assertive.

The first step in learning to use assertive discipline is to recognize and remove these roadblocks. Most of them have to do with *negative expectations about students*: We expect them to act bad. We feel that their health, home, personality, or environment prohibit their behaving acceptably in school. Victor has a history of hyperactivity; Stacy may be a victim of child abuse; no one has ever been able to do a thing with Donald. Therefore we do not expect that they can behave. This negative expectation must be recognized as false, and it must be supplanted with positive expectations.

The second thing teachers must do is recognize the simple fact that *they can influence in positive ways the behavior of all students under their direction, no matter what the problems.* Recognition of this fact helps remove the roadblocks associated with negative expectations. Teachers should focus on the following realities:

1. *All students need limits, and teachers have the right to set them.* Teachers who fear that students will not like them if they set limits and stick to them have not paid attention to human psychology. We admire and respect teachers who hold high expectations and high standards. We seldom respect teachers if they take a laissez-faire approach to teaching.
2. *Teachers have the right to ask for and receive backup help from principals, parents, and other school personnel.* Teachers who have such support will not be intimidated when students behave defiantly or hostilely.
3. *We can't always treat all students exactly alike.* Teachers have heard that standards and consequences must be applied equally to all students. This is true up to a point. However, students respond differently within given situations. They realize that sometimes their peers need special help, and they are accepting and understanding when a special incentives program or behavior modification is used for certain students.

Step 2. Practice The Use of Assertive Response Styles

Canter differentiates among three styles of responses that characterize teachers' interactions with misbehaving students: (1) *nonassertive*, (2) *hostile*, and (3) *assertive*. The first two should be eliminated, while the third should be practiced and implemented. Here is how Canter describes them:

Nonassertive Response Style. The nonassertive response style is typical of teachers who have given in to students or who feel it is wrong to place strong demands on student behavior. Terry and Rick are talking, giggling, and engaging in horseplay that has almost ruined the lesson. Miss Jenkins looks up and says, "For the tenth time, would you two *please* stop that?" She continues the lesson, and within a few minutes the two boys are disrupting again.

Teachers using this nonassertive style are passive. They either do not establish clear standards or else they fail to back up their standards with appropriate actions. They hope their good natures will gain student compliance. They often ask students to "please try" to do their work, or behave themselves, or do better next time. They are not firm or insistent, and they end up resignedly accepting whatever the students decide to do.

Hostile Response Style. Miss Jenkins finally reaches the end of her rope with Terry and Rick. She yells, "All right, you two! That's the last straw! You either pay attention or you are going to regret it!"

The hostile response style is used by teachers who feel that they are barely hanging on to class control. They use aversive techniques such as sarcasm and threats. They often shout. They believe they must rule with an iron fist or else they will be overwhelmed with chaos. Hostile responses produce several bad side effects—they hurt students' feelings; they provoke disrespect and desire to get even; they fail to meet students' needs for warmth and security; and they violate two of the basic student rights described earlier: the right to positive limits on self-destructive behavior and the right to choose their own behavior, with full knowledge of the consequences that will follow.

Assertive Response Style. Terry and Rick are now in Miss Beech's class. They are talking and playing during the lesson. Miss Beech looks directly at them, writes their names on the board, and says "It is against the rules for you to talk without permission during the lesson." The boys know that having their names on the board is a warning. The lesson resumes and so does their misbehavior. Miss Beech makes a check mark beside each of their names. They know that the class rules now require that they spend 15 minutes in detention, and that Miss Beech always follows through to back up the rules.

The assertive response style, which should be practiced until it becomes a natural in dealing with students, protects the rights of both teacher and students. With this style, teachers make their expectations clearly known to students. In a businesslike way they continually insist that students comply with those expectations. They back up their words with actions. When students choose to comply with teacher guidance, they receive positive benefits. When they choose to behave in unacceptable ways, the teacher follows through with consequences that reasonably accompany the misbehavior (Davidman & Davidman, 1984).

Examples of Nonassertive, Hostile, and Assertive Responses

Example: Fighting
- Nonassertive: Please try your very best to stop fighting.
- Hostile: You are acting like disgusting savages!
- Assertive: We do not fight. Sit down until you cool off.

Example: Talking Out
- Nonassertive: You are talking again without raising your hand.
- Hostile: Learn some manners or else there's going to be trouble!

- Assertive: Don't answer unless you raise your hand and I call on you.

Notice in these examples that the assertive response clearly communicates the teacher's disapproval of the behavior, followed by an indication of what the student is supposed to do. In contrast, the nonassertive response leaves students unconvinced that they are truly expected to behave differently; it suggests that the teacher is afraid or feels powerless. The hostile response is counterproductive in that it wounds students; it smacks of dislike and vengeance and depicts the classroom as a battleground where teacher and students are adversaries. If the threats are not carried out, they quickly lose their effect. But if they are carried out, distrust of the teacher and desire for revenge rapidly grow.

Step 3. Learning to Set Limits

Canter makes this point clearly: "No matter what the activity, in order to be assertive, you need to be aware of what behaviors you want and need from the students" (1976, p. 65). He would have teachers identify the specific behaviors they expect from students, such as taking turns, not shouting out, starting work on time, and listening to another student who is speaking. Following this identification, teachers should then instruct their students very clearly on the behaviors they have identified. It is often helpful to make very succinct lists of dos and don'ts, as well as specific directions and reminders, that can be posted in the room. All of these refer to setting limits.

Once the specific behaviors are made explicit, the next step in limit setting is to decide how to follow through for both compliance and noncompliance. For compliance, verbal acknowledgment is usually sufficient. Sometimes special rewards and privileges may be given. Dealing with noncompliance is more difficult, and it is here that assertive discipline is most effective. When preparing to deal with inappropriate behaviors, teachers should be ready with firm reminders of what students are supposed to be doing. Canter goes into detail in describing verbal limit setting, emphasizing three techniques:

1. *Requesting appropriate behavior*, which is done by means of
   Hints—statements made from time to time to remind students of what they are supposed to be doing (e.g., "Everyone should be reading silently.")
   I–messages—telling students how behavior is affecting the teacher (e.g., "It is getting so noisy I can't do my work.")

Questions—hints put into interrogative form (e.g., "Would you please get back to your reading?")

Demands—statements that direct students on what to do (e.g., "Get back to your reading right now.") Canter warns of the negative effects that demands can have, and here issues his only commandment concerning assertive discipline: *Thou shalt not make a demand thou art not preparest to follow through on.*

2. *Delivering the verbal limit,* which has to do with tone of voice, eye contact, gestures, and so forth:

Tone of voice—should be firmly neutral and business-like. Should not be harsh, abusive, sarcastic, or intimidating. Neither should it be mirthful, implying a lack of seriousness.

Eye contact—For a message to have greatest impact, teachers should look students straight in the eye. However, teachers should not insist that students look them back in the eye. Even though students look away, teachers should fix them with a direct gaze when verbally setting limits.

Gestures—add much to verbal messages, especially in Anglo-American society, where few gestures are used. Facial expressions and arm and hand movements accentuate messages. However, Canter cautions that fingers and fists should not be waved in students' faces.

Use of students' names—adds further impact to verbal messages, making them more forceful and penetrating. This is especially true for messages delivered over longer distances, as across the room or school grounds.

Physical touch—Touch is unusually effective in conjunction with verbal messages. Light hand placement on the shoulder powerfully communicates forcefulness combined with sincerity. Canter warns, however, that some students react violently to touches, by pulling away abruptly or even thrusting back. They may also claim that the teacher has pinched or hurt them.

3. *Using the broken record technique,* which involves insistent repetition of the original message, especially effective when students seek to divert teachers from their intended message. Here is an example:

TEACHER: Alex, we do not fight in this room. I will not tolerate fighting. You must not fight again.

STUDENT: It's not my fault. Pete started it. He hit me first.

TEACHER: I understand that might be. I didn't see. But you will not fight in my class.

STUDENT: Well Pete started it.

TEACHER: That may be. I'll watch. But you *may not fight in this class.*

The broken record technique (repetition that we do not fight in this class) maintained firm, positive insistence. Canter gives these reminders concerning its use:

1. Use it only when students refuse to listen, persist in responding inappropriately, or refuse to take responsibility for their own behavior.
2. Preface your repetitions with, "That's not the point..." or "I understand, but..."
3. Use it a maximum of three times; after the third time follow through with an appropriate consequence, if necessary (1976, p. 88).

Step 4. Learning to Follow Through on Limits

By "limits" Canter means the positive demands you have made on students. By "following through" he means the appropriate actions you take both when students comply (positive results) and when they fail to comply (negative results). The students have already been carefully informed that consequences, good or bad, will follow the behavior they choose. Canter presents the following guidelines for following through appropriately:

1. *Make promises, not threats.* A promise is a vow to take appropriate action when necessary. A threat is a statement that shows intent to harm or punish. Students know what is expected of them. They can choose to behave as expected or they can choose to behave undesirably. In either case the consequence comes not as a surprise out of the blue, but as a promise the teacher has made in advance.
2. *Select appropriate consequences in advance.* Teachers should select several specific consequences that can be invoked when necessary. They should be both positive and negative, with gradations of severity for violations of the rules. Examples of negative consequences that teachers have found most useful are time out, loss of privilege, loss of preferred activity, detention, visit to the principal, and being sent home from school. All of the consequences, both positive and negative, should indicate that teachers truly care about the students and their behavior, and that they are always disposed to influencing their behavior in positive directions.
3. *Set up a system of consequences that you can easily enforce.* Canter suggests the following, but emphasizes that individual teachers must

come up with their own systems with which they feel comfortable. (These are for individual students, starting at the beginning of the day or period. Each new day begins afresh.)

Misbehavior	*Consequence*
first	name on board (a warning)
second	check by name (15 minutes detention after or in-school)
third	second check (30 minutes detention after or in-school)
fourth	third check (30 minutes detention; student phones parents and explains)
fifth	fourth check (30 minutes detention; student phones parents, explains, and meets with the principal)
sixth	student suspended; taken home by principal, vice-principal, or counselor.

4. *Practice verbal confrontations that call for follow through.* The only way to begin to use assertions and consequences naturally is to practice them, preferably in advance rather than whenever the situation might arise in the classroom. One good way to practice is to follow this sequence:

   a. Describe a rule to your imaginary class, such as "No talking out without permission." You briefly explain why it is necessary, what students should do instead, and what the consequences will be for compliance and noncompliance.

   b. Imagine that a student has talked out. Make an assertive response. Suppose the student talks back. Use the broken record technique. Suppose the student still talks back. Assertively state the consequence. Suppose the student defies you. Follow through assertively. (Refer to the suggestions given above.)

Step 5. Implementing a System of Positive Consequences

The previous section emphasized negative assertions and consequences, because they are what teachers are most concerned with and with which they feel least adequate. However, the positive side of the picture is, according the Canter, even more important to good discipline. This involves what you do to or for students when they behave appropriately, and it builds influence you have with students, decreases the amount of problem behavior, and makes the classroom much more positive overall. Here are some of the positive consequences suggested as effective by Canter.

1. *Personal attention from the teacher.* Special, positive, personal attention from the teacher is one of the most rewarding experiences

that students can have. Most students respond enthusiastically to that attention. It is given in the form of greetings, short talks, compliments, acknowledgments, smiles, and friendly eye contact.

2. *Positive notes to parents.* Parents are usually informed about their children only when they have misbehaved in school. A brief note or phone call, positive and complimentary, can do wonders for both students and parents. They also rally parents to the support of teachers.

3. *Special awards.* Students respond well to special awards given for high achievement, significant improvement, and so forth. Younger students love them. Secondary students' reactions are less predictable, since they are so strongly influenced by peers' responses to them. This can be discussed with older students before being used.

4. *Special privileges.* Students of all ages respond well to special privileges, such as helping take care of classroom animals or equipment, helping with class materials, or working together with a friend.

5. *Material rewards.* Many tangible objects are effective rewards. Young students like stickers, badges, ribbons, etc. Older students like to receive posters, pencils, rubber stamps, etc.

6. *Home rewards.* In collaboration with parents, privileges can be extended to the home. Completing homework can earn extra television time, reading an extra book can earn a favorite meal, and so forth.

7. *Group rewards.* Canter discusses methods of rewarding the entire group for good behavior. He includes suggestions such as: (1) dropping marbles into a jar, as the entire group remains on task and works hard (when the jar is filled, the class earns something special); and (2) writing a series of letters of the alphabet on the board that when completed make up a secret word, such as POPCORN PARTY, which the class then receives as a reward (1976, pp. 122–126).

BEGINNING THE YEAR

Although an assertive discipline program can be implemented at any time, the first few days of a new school year are an especially good time to introduce the program. Canter suggests the following:

1. Decide on behaviors you want from students, together with the positive and negative consequences.

2. Take your list to the principal for approval and support.
3. At the first meeting with the new students, discuss the behaviors, consequences, and methods of follow through you intend to use. Keep the list of behaviors (rules) to six or less.
4. Stress that no student will be allowed to break the rules. Tell the students exactly what will happen each time a rule is broken (first, second, third offense, etc.).
5. Ask the students to write the behaviors and consequences on a sheet of paper, take the plan home, have their parents read and sign it, and return it the next day.
6. Emphasize repeatedly that these rules will help the class toward its responsibility of learning and behaving acceptably.
7. Ask students to repeat orally what is expected and what will happen for compliance and for violations.
8. Prepare a short letter concerning the plan to go home to parents, indicating your need for their support and your pleasure in collaborating with them toward the benefit of their child.
9. Implement the assertive discipline plan immediately (1976, pp. 136–139).

COMMENTS ON CANTER'S MODEL

You can see that Canter's model of assertive discipline integrates within its scope ideas and techniques from several other models, such as behavior as choice, logical consequences rather than threats or punishments, positive reinforcement for desired behavior, addressing the situation rather than the student's character, and so forth. However, it is unique in several ways—in its overall ease of implementation, its insistence on meeting teachers' and students' rights in the classroom, its emphasis on caring enough about students to limit their self-defeating behavior, and its insisting on support from administrators and parents.

In addition to these qualities, it provides something that teachers prize greatly: it effectively stops misbehavior while allowing teachers to go ahead teaching. Teachers don't have to suffer the agony of verbal confrontations with students, nor do they have to give up the large amounts of instructional time required by other systems of discipline. Those qualities have caused assertive discipline to be one of the most widely-accepted systems of discipline now available to teachers.

Does it, then, have shortcomings? Many teachers find fault with it. Among the complaints one hears are that it is too harsh, too militant, too overpowering for young children, too demeaning to older students, too focused on suppressing bad behavior to the exclusion of building values for good, responsible behavior. As with anything else, people have different opinions; nothing pleases everyone all the time. All in all, however, the widespread popularity of assertive discipline speaks for itself.

Application Exercises

CASE #1. KRIS WILL NOT WORK:

Kris, a student in Mr. Jake's class is quite docile. She socializes little with other students and never disrupts lessons. However, despite Mr. Jake's best efforts, Kris will not do her work. She rarely completes and assignment. She is simply there, like a bump on a log, putting forth no effort at all.

How would Canter deal with Kris? Canter would advise Mr. Jake to do the following:

1. Clearly communicate the class expectations to Kris, in assertively unmistakable terms.
2. Use a firm tone of voice and eye contact when reminding Kris of the expectations.
3. Consistently follow through with preestablished consequences. Make the negative consequences more severe and the positive consequences more attractive until finding a level that works for Kris.
4. Contact Kris's parents about her behavior. Explain that it is in Kris's best interest that the parents and Mr. Jake work together to help Kris.

CASE #2. TOM IS HOSTILE AND DEFIANT:

Tom has appeared to be in his usual foul mood ever since arriving in class. He gets up and on his way to sharpen his pencil he bumps into Frank. Frank complains. Tom tells him loudly to shut up. Miss Baines, the teacher, says "Tom, go back to your seat." Tom wheels around, swears loudly and says heatedly "I'll go when I'm damned good and ready!"

How would Canter suggest that Miss Baines deal with Tom?

ACTIVITIES:

A. Each of the following exemplifies an important point in Canter's model of discipline. Identify the point illustrated by each.
    1. Miss Hatcher, on seeing her class list for the coming year, exclaims "Oh no! Billy Smythe in my class! There goes my sanity!"
    2. "If you talk again during the class, you will have to stay an extra five minutes."
    3. "I understand what you are saying, but you may not curse in this room."
    4. "How many times do I have to tell you not to talk?"
    5. If a student receives a third check, he or she must go to the office and call his or her parent to explain what has happened.

6. If the class is especially attentive and hardworking, they earn five minutes for visiting at the end of the period.
7. "If you talk again during the class, I guarantee you will regret it!"

B. For a grade level and/or subject your select, outline an assertive discipline plan that includes:
1. Four rules.
2. Positive and negative consequences associated with the rules.
3. The people you will inform about your system, and how you will inform them.

REFERENCES

Canter, L. (1976). *Assertive discipline: a take-charge approach for today's educator.* Seal Beach, CA: Canter and Associates.

Canter, L. (1978). Be an assertive teacher. *Instructor, 88,* 60.

Davidman, L., & Davidman, P. (1984). Logical assertion: a rationale and strategy [suggestions for teachers based on the Canter assertive discipline program]. *Educational Forum, 48,* 165–176.

CHAPTER 8

The Glasser Model:
Good Behavior Comes from Good Choices and Meeting Needs

GLASSER BIOGRAPHICAL SKETCH

William Glasser, a Los Angeles psychiatrist, was born in Cleveland, Ohio, in 1925. He first became a chemical engineer, but later turned to psychology and then to psychiatry. For over 30 years he has worked with correctional agencies, helped develop programs for school districts, and lectured widely about his ideas for working with school students.

Glasser has received national acclaim in both psychiatry and education. His book *Reality Therapy: A New Approach to Psychiatry* (1965) shifted a long-standing focus in treating behavior problems. Instead of seeking to uncover the conditions in one's past that contributed to inappropriate behavior (the psychoanalytic approach), Glasser directs attention to the present, to the reality of the situation. He believes that it is what one does right now that matters and that this present reality is what psychiatrists should concern themselves with.

Glasser extended his ideas from reality therapy to the school arena. His work with juvenile offenders further convinced him that teachers could help students make better choices about their school behavior. Glasser insisted that teachers should never excuse bad student behavior. Poor background or undesirable living conditions do not exempt students from their responsibility to learn and behave properly in school. This point of view together with practical advice for carrying it out forms the core of Glasser's book *Schools Without Failure* (1969), acknowledged to be one of the most influential educational books of all time.

In 1985 Glasser published a book entitled *Control Theory in the Classroom*, in which he gives a different emphasis to his contentions concerning discipline. This emphasis is encapsulated in his pronouncement that if students are to continue working and behaving properly, they must "believe that if they do some work, they will be able to satisfy their needs enough so that it makes sense to keep working." Thus, Glasser has given much more emphasis than previously to the school's role in meeting basic student needs, as a prime factor in discipline and work output. Because of the rather different emphases in Glasser's earlier and later works, his model of discipline is presented in two parts—pre–1985 and post–1985.

GLASSER'S MAIN FOCUSES

Glasser's work in school discipline now has two main focuses. The first is on providing a classroom environment and curriculum that meets students' basic needs for belonging, power, fun, and freedom, as a means of motivating students and reducing misbehavior. The second focus is on helping students make good behavioral choices that lead ultimately to personal success.

GLASSER: PRE-1985

Key Ideas

1. Students are rational beings. They can control their behavior. They choose to act the way they do.
2. Good choices produce good behavior. Bad choices produce bad behavior.
3. Teachers must always try to help students make good choices.
4. Teachers who truly care about their students accept no excuses for bad behavior.
5. Reasonable consequences should always follow student behavior, good or bad.
6. Class rules are essential and they must be enforced.
7. Classroom meetings are effective vehicles for attending to matters of class rules, behavior, and discipline.

GLASSER'S FUNDAMENTAL VIEWS

Glasser's pre-1985 views about discipline were simple, yet powerful. Behavior is a matter of choice. Good behavior results from good choices and bad behavior results from bad choices. A student's duty is to make good choices. A teacher's duty is to help students make those good choices.

Psychologists and educators often look into students' backgrounds for underlying causes of misbehavior. You often hear teachers say, "What can you expect? Juan comes from a broken home," or "Sara was an abused child," or "Eddie's family lives in poverty." Glasser does not deny that such conditions exist or that they influence behavior. He simply says that humans, unlike dogs and parakeets, have rational minds and can make rational choices. They can understand what acceptable school behavior is and can choose to behave in acceptable ways.

But in order to make good choices students must come to see the results of those choices as desirable. If bad behavior choices get them what they want, they will make bad choices. That is where the teacher comes in—helping students see that they are choosing to act in the ways they do. The teacher forces them to acknowledge their behavior and make value judgments about it. The teacher refuses to accept excuses for bad behavior, always directing attention instead to what would be more acceptable. The essence of discipline, then, is in helping students make good choices.

WHAT SCHOOL OFFERS

Prior to 1985, Glasser contended that schools offer students a good chance to be successful and to be recognized. Indeed, for many students schools offered the only opportunities to meet those needs. Success in school produces a sense of self-worth and a success identity, which mitigate deviant behavior. The road to a success identity begins with a good relationship with people who care. For students who come from atrocious backgrounds, school may be the only place to find a person genuinely interested in them.

Yet students often resist entering into quality relationships. They may fear teachers, distrust adults in general, or obtain peer rewards by disdaining teachers. Teachers must therefore be very persistent, never waning in their efforts to help students. Glasser maintains that students cannot begin to make better, more responsible choices until they become deeply involved emotionally with people who can make such choices, people such as teachers.

WHAT TEACHERS SHOULD DO

Glasser (1978) firmly believes that teachers hold the key to good discipline. He concludes that both teachers and students have important roles to play in maintaining effective discipline, but today he puts much greater responsibility on the shoulders of teachers than he formerly did. He has always maintained that the following actions are the teacher's responsibility.

1. Stress Student Responsibility

Since good behavior comes from good choices and since students ultimately must live with the choices they make, their responsibility for their own behavior is always kept in the forefront.

Discussions in which this responsibility is explored and clarified occur in classroom meetings. These meetings occur as regular parts of the curriculum. Students sit in a tight circle with the teacher and discuss matters that concern the class.

Today, for example, Mr. Davies' class meeting focuses on a discussion of what should be done about students who fail to bring needed materials to class. Several students suggest positive solutions, and the group decides to try one of them. On subsequent days Mr. Davies calls attention directly and indirectly to the responsibilities in the solution suggested in the class-room meeting. This accomplishes two things: First, attention emphasizes that good behavior comes from good choices that students can and should make. Second, attention cements the caring bond between teacher and student. Bit by bit the message gets through that the teacher truly cares about students and their behavior.

2. Establish Rules that Lead to Success

Glasser considers class rules to be essential. He writes disparagingly of pro-grams and classes that attempt to operate without rules, in the mistaken be-lief that rules stifle initiative, responsibility, and self-direction. He stresses that rules are essential especially for students who have done poorly in school. Permissiveness for those students tends to be destructive. It fosters antagonism, ridicule, and lack of respect for teachers and others.

Rules should be established by teachers and students together and should facilitate personal and group achievement. Rules should be adapted to the age, ability, and other realities of the students.

Mrs. Bentley's second graders decide on these rules:

1. Always listen to the teacher.
2. Raise your hand to talk.
3. Finish all your work.
4. Be kind to others.

Mr. Jason's ninth grade physical education class decided on these:

1. Be on time.
2. Play safely.
3. Practice sportsmanship.
4. Take care of equipment.

One thing is essential: Rules must always reinforce the basic idea that students are in school to study and learn. Furthermore, rules should con-stantly be evaluated to see whether they are useful. When no longer useful, they should be discarded or changed. So long as they are retained, how-ever, they must be enforced.

3. Accept No Excuses

For discipline to be successful, teachers must accept no excuses. Glasser uses this "no excuse" dictum in two areas. The first has to do with condi-tions outside the school. What goes on there does not excuse bad behavior in school. Those conditions may, indeed, cause bad behavior, but that does not make it acceptable. The teacher must never say, "We can excuse Bill's behavior today because he has had trouble at home. It is okay if he yells and hits."

The second area in which Glasser says teachers should accept no excuses concerns student commitment. Once a student has decided on a course of good behavior and has made a commitment to it, the teacher must never accept excuses for the student's failing to live up to that commitment. A teacher who accepts an excuse says, in effect, that it is all right to break a commitment, that it is all right for students to harm themselves. Teachers who care, Glasser says, accept no excuses.

4. Call for Value Judgments

When students exhibit inappropriate behavior, teachers should have them make value judgments about it. Glasser (1977) suggests the following procedure when a student is misbehaving:

TEACHER: "What are you doing?" (Asked in unthreatening tone of voice.)
STUDENT: (Will usually give an honest answer if not threatened.)
TEACHER: "Is that helping you or the class?"
STUDENT: "No."
TEACHER: "What could you do that would help?"
STUDENT: (Names better behavior; if can think of none, teacher suggests appropriate alternatives and lets student choose.)

Sometimes the student does not respond in an acceptable way, but instead replies hostilely or caustically. For that eventuality, Glasser presents the following scenario:

1. Student is misbehaving.

TEACHER: What are you doing? Is it against the rules? What should you be doing?
STUDENT: (Responds negatively, unacceptably.)
TEACHER: I would like to talk with you privately at (specifies time).

2. Private conference between teacher and student.

TEACHER: What were you doing? Was it against the rules? What should you have been doing?
STUDENT: (Agrees to proper course of behavior.)

3. Student later repeats the misbehavior. Teacher calls for another private conference.

TEACHER: We have to work this out. What kind of plan can you make so you can follow the rules?

STUDENT: I'll stop doing it.

TEACHER: No, we need a plan that says exactly what you *will do*. Let's make a simple plan you can follow. I'll help you.

4. Student later repeats misbehavior; does not abide by own plan. Teacher assigns "time out." This is isolation from the group. Student is not allowed to participate with the group again until making a commitment to the teacher to adhere to the plan. If student disrupts during time out, he is excluded from the class-room. (A contingency plan should be set up in advance with the principal.)

5. Student, after returning to the group, disrupts again.

TEACHER: Things are not working out here for you and me. We have tried hard. You must leave the class. As soon as you have a plan you are sure will allow you to follow the rules of the class, let me know. We can try again. But for now, please report to the principal's office. (Principal was informed in advance of this possibility.)

6. If student is out of control, principal notifies parents and asks them to pick up student at school immediately.

7. Students who are repeatedly sent home are referred to a special school or class, or to a different community agency.

By following this procedure consistently, teachers can cause students to doubt the value of their misbehavior, make responsible and better choices, and thus gradually make a commitment to choosing behaviors that bring personal success instead of failure.

5. Suggest Suitable Alternatives

First grader Alonzo has been having trouble lining up promptly when the bell rings. Ms. Stafford offered him these two choices: Either (1) get in line immediately when the bell rings, or (2) be last to go out for recess. Alonzo chose number one. He understands that he is expected to live by his choice, and Ms. Stafford helps him remember that.

Misbehaving students will sometimes be unable to think of appropriate behaviors they might select. The teacher should then suggest two or three acceptable alternatives. The student chooses one of the alternatives and is expected to abide by the choice made. This strengthens the concept of choice linked to responsibility. The teacher accepts no excuses for failure to abide by the choice, although if the choice proves untenable the student is allowed to make another choice.

6. Invoke Reasonable Consequences

Glasser stresses that reasonable consequences must follow whatever behavior the student chooses. These consequences will be desirable if good behavior is chosen and undesirable if poor behavior is chosen. Never should teachers manipulate events so that these consequences do not occur. If the student consciously selects an inappropriate behavior that calls for, let us say, isolation from the group, then isolation should occur promptly without exception. These consequences should not be physically punishing, nor should they employ caustic language, ridicule, or sarcasm. However, they must be unpleasant to the student. On the other hand, consequences of good behavior should be pleasant and personally satisfying.

The knowledge that behavior always brings consequences and that individuals can largely choose behavior that brings pleasant as opposed to unpleasant consequences builds the sense that people are in charge of their own lives and in control of their own behavior.

7. Be Persistent

Caring teachers work toward one major goal—getting students to commit themselves to desirable courses of behavior. Commitment means constancy, doing something repeatedly, intentionally, while making sure that it is right. It does not mean doing the thing part of the time and not doing it part of the time.

To convey this idea and help implant it in students, teachers themselves must be constant. They must always help students make choices and have them make value judgments about their bad choices. They must always see tomorrow as a new day and be willing to start again. In short, caring teachers never give up in helping their students toward self-discipline. Even when progress is slow, they persevere because they know it is the student's best hope for ultimately gaining maturity, respect, and success identity.

8. Carry Out Continual Review

For Glasser, the *classroom meeting* is central to implementation of a good system of discipline. A classroom meeting allows a discussion of topics relevant to the students by the entire class. It explores problems and suggests solutions; it does not place blame on anyone. It is carried out with students and teacher seated in a closed circle, an arrangement that has come to be known as the Glasser Circle.

Glasser advocates three types of classroom meetings: (1) *social problem solving*, (2) *educational diagnostic*, and (3) *open ended*. He would have them all be a regular part of the curriculum. The first type attempts to solve problems that arise among people living and working within the school setting. It is a natural place to consider matters related to discipline. The second type has to do with problems of curriculum, instructional activities, and learning. The third deals with any topic of concern to the students.

Discussions in classroom meetings focus on two things: (1) identifying the problem, and (2) seeking solutions to the problem. Students are never allowed to find fault with others, place blame on them, or seek to punish them. The teacher remains in the background during the discussion, giving opinions sparingly and participating in a way that reflects student attitudes back to the group for examination. Glasser stresses that the meetings require practice before they will be successful, and that unless they are focused on finding solutions, they will not produce the desired effect.

COMMENTS ON GLASSER: PRE–1985

In Glasser's earlier work, he cast the school in quite a positive light. While acknowledging that problems existed for some students, he steadfastly maintained that schools afforded students the best—often the *only*—opportunity to associate with quality adults who genuinely cared about them. Schools therefore offered students the best opportunity many would ever have for finding belonging, success, and positive self-identity. In order to take advantage of this crucial opportunity, students were continually asked to make value judgments about their misbehavior, urged to make good choices and plans that improve the chances for good choices, and confronted with the consequences of their good and bad choices.

As you will see in the material that follows, Glasser now places much greater onus on the schools. Schools, he maintains, should be refocused in terms of student needs and the meeting of those needs, rather than molding students to deal with the conditions that they encounter in schools.

GLASSER: POST–1985

Key Ideas

1. All of our behavior is our best attempt to control ourselves to meet our needs.
2. We always choose to do what is most satisfying to us at the time.
3. All of us have inborn needs that we continually attempt to satisfy. Included among those inborn needs are:
   a. to belong

    b. to gain power

    c. to be free

    d. to have fun.

4. We feel pleasure when these needs are met, and frustration when they are not.
5. We feel a continual urge to act when any need is unsatisfied.
6. If schools are to have good discipline, they must create classes in which fewer students and teachers are frustrated.
7. Only a discipline program that is concerned with classroom satisfaction will work. That means that students must feel they belong, have some power, have a sense of freedom, and have fun in learning.

THE REFOCUS ON STUDENT NEEDS

For one who long and staunchly maintained that it was a students' responsibility to make choices that brought success, Glasser's recent assertions that discipline depends on schools' meeting students' needs seems a rather sharp turnabout. What could have prompted so important a redirecting, a refocusing on the nexus of classroom discipline?

Glasser's newer views on discipline have occurred as a direct extension of his conclusions concerning the condition of schooling at the secondary level. He maintains that "no more than half of our secondary school students are willing to make an effort to learn, and therefore cannot be taught" (1985, p. 3). This is true despite dedicated teachers' best efforts, and therefore "I believe that we have gone as far as we can go with the traditional structure of our secondary schools" (1985, p. 6).

Glasser's conclusions are shared by many, if not most secondary teachers, who are pleased to work with dedicated, high achieving students, but terribly frustrated in working with the 50% (many of whom are quite intelligent) who do not even try to learn. Many secondary teachers report that their main discipline problems are not defiance or disruption, but overwhelming apathy and benign unwillingness to participate in classroom activities and assignments.

How does Glasser account for this situation? Consider his description of a good school, which he defines as "a place where almost all students believe that if they do some work, they will be able to satisfy their needs enough so that it makes sense to keep trying (1985, p. 15). Glasser maintains that most schools do not meet students' needs to a level sufficient to keep more than half of them involved with the curriculum.

And what are those needs that are not being met? Glasser emphasizes four of them, which he contends are genetically inborn and cannot be denied even by students who would try:

1. *The need to belong*, to feel accepted, to be a member of the group or class.
2. *The need for power*, not so much power over others as power to control part of one's own life and power to do things competently.
3. *The need for freedom*, to feel at least partly in control of self, self-reliant, without constant direction from others.
4. *The need for fun*, for enjoyment, for pleasure, for satisfaction.

Glasser would have schools recognize these four fundamental needs that play powerful roles in student behavior, recognize that students cannot deny those needs and must try to fulfill them, and recognize that schooling can and should be restructured in such a manner that it will meet those needs for most students. Glasser contends that such a restructuring would recapture half of the 50% of high school students who are now disengaged from formal education. In short, students would work in school because the work helps meet their needs and they therefore find it satisfying.

HOW DOES THIS RELATE TO DISCIPLINE?

Glasser makes a provocative statement that is eloquently simple. He says that if a student does not work in class, we can safely assume that the classwork is less satisfying than whatever the student happens to be doing. Often what the student does is sit and daydream, or look out the window, or doodle with pencil and paper. Sometimes the student talks to others or walks about the room, acts generally considered to be behavior problems. Occasionally, they talk out loudly, speak sarcastically, and call each other names. According to Glasser, they do that because it brings them more satisfaction than working in and successfully completing the class activities.

Previously, Glasser would have contended that the fault lay mostly with the unattending students, that they could choose to do the work, that they could gain a sense of success by doing so, and that they could gradually come to value, or at least comply with, the work required. Now Glasser expresses a different view:

> When we talk about better discipline with no attempt to create a more satisfying school, what we are really talking about is getting disruptive students to turn off a biological control system that they cannot turn off. We are asking for the impossible when we look for ways to make students who are not satisfied stop trying to get what they want through behaviors like disrupting, using drugs or creative 'dyslexic' nonreading behaviors. *This is like asking someone who is sitting on a hot stove to sit still and stop complaining* (1985, p. 53, italics added).

Glasser goes on to say that in classrooms where there is little needs satisfaction, students will not sit and wait because they have learned that there is little payoff for patience. He concludes this point by stating that "Teachers should not depend on any discipline program that demands that they do something *to* or *for* students to get them to stop behaving badly in unsatisfying classes. Only a discipline program that is also concerned with classroom satisfaction will work" (1985, p. 56).

GLASSER'S PROPOSED SOLUTION

Glasser believes that unsatisfying classrooms can be made better almost at once, by teachers moving from traditional structure to having students work together in small learning teams. He feels small learning groups of about four in number offer the following advantages:

1. Sense of belonging for all students.
2. Motivation for students to work on behalf of the group.
3. Stronger students meet their needs for power and friendships by helping weaker students in the group.
4. Weaker students have needs met by contributing to the group.
5. Students are freed from overdependence on the teacher; they help each other.

He contrasts these advantages with traditional classroom organization in which:

1. Students work as individuals.
2. Unless students are achievers, there is little motivation to work.
3. Weaker students contribute little to the class.
4. Dependence on the teacher is unduly high.
5. Student boredom is high; bored students will not work.

Glasser advocates learning teams because they better meet students' needs and therefore increase work output while reducing discipline problems. If they accomplish what he suggests, they would be well worth using for those reasons alone. However, research is accumulating quite rapidly that shows that cooperative learning (i.e., learning by classroom teams as advocated by Glasser) produces significantly better overall educational results than does individual learning. That research evidence, together with directions for using cooperative learning, is presented in greater detail in Chapter 9.

COMMENTS ON GLASSER'S MODEL

Glasser's work prior to 1985 furnished what was once considered to be his model of discipline. The new ideas he has set forth in *Control Theory in the Classroom* seem at first unrelated to his earlier work on discipline, or even opposed to it. One wonders whether the later work is intended to replace the earlier work.

Glasser has not provided an answer to this question, but on reflection the complementary nature of the earlier and later work becomes evident. It is reasonable to conclude that Glasser would have teachers *begin* with organizing their classes so as to meet students' needs to the extent possible. But he concedes that probably about 25% of the secondary students will still be unproductive. And of course even productive students often present discipline problems.

Once the class is better organized to meet students' needs, then Glasser's earlier suggestions on how to deal with misbehaving students are still appropriate. Simple improvement in meeting student needs, while tremendously important, does not do away with all misbehavior. Students therefore should still be helped to see that good behavior choices lead to better results. They should still be urged to show responsibility for their actions and to be considerate of others. Thus, Glasser's model of discipline can now be seen in this expanded form—first organize the class to meet needs as well as possible, then continue to use the intervention strategies for controlling and improving behavior.

Application Exercises

CASE #1. KRIS WILL NOT WORK:

Kris, a student in Mr. Jake's class, is quite docile. She socializes little with other students and never disrupts class. However, despite Mr. Jake's best efforts, Kris never does her work. She rarely completes an assignment. She is simply there, like a bump on a log, putting forth no effort.

How would Glasser deal with Kris? Glasser would first suggest that Mr. Jake think carefully about the classroom and the program to try to determine whether they contain obstacles that prevent Kris from meeting her needs for belonging, fun, power, and freedom. He would have Mr. Jake talk directly with Kris about this matter. If changes are needed for her, Mr. Jake should make them if possible.

If no changes seem warranted, Glasser would have Mr. Jake talk with Kris so as to accomplish the following:

1. Make sure Kris understands her work responsibilities as a student in the class.

2. Make sure Kris understands that she can choose her behavior—to work or not—and that her choice brings with it either desirable or undesirable consequences.
3. Accept no excuses from Kris for not beginning and completing her work.
4. Help Kris identify some alternative behaviors from which she can choose.
5. Continually press Kris to make value judgments about her choice of behavior.
6. Make sure that when Kris shows improvement, she receives consequences that are very attractive to her.
7. Never give up on Kris.

CASE #2. TOM IS HOSTILE AND DEFIANT:

Tom has appeared to be in his usual foul mood ever since arriving in class. He gets up and on his way to sharpen his pencil he bumps into Frank. Frank complains. Tom tells him loudly to shut up. Miss Baines, the teacher, says "Tom, go back to your seat." Tom wheels around, swears loudly and says heatedly, "I'll go when I'm damned good and ready!"

How would Glasser have Miss Baines deal with Tom?

ACTIVITIES:

1. Select a preferred grade level and/or subject. As the teacher, outline what you would consider and do, along the lines of Glasser's suggestions, concerning:
   (a) Organizing the classroom, class, curriculum, and activities so as better to meet your students' needs for belonging, fun, power, and freedom.
   (b) Your continual efforts to help students make work and personal behavior choices that have a good chance of bringing them success.
2. Do a comparative analysis of Glasser's system of discipline with those of Canter and Jones, in terms of:
   (a) Effectiveness in suppressing inappropriate behavior;
   (b) Effectiveness in building long-lasting better behavior;
   (c) Ease of implementation;
   (d) Effect on student self-concept;
   (e) Effect on bonds of trust between teacher and student.
3. Outline how you might combine elements from the models of Glasser, Canter, and Jones so as to make a system of discipline that is more effective than any one of those models by itself.

REFERENCES

Glasser, W. (1965). *Reality therapy: a new approach to psychiatry.* New York: Harper and Row.

Glasser, W. (1969). *Schools without failure*. New York: Harper and Row.

Glasser, W. (1977). 10 steps to good discipline, *Today's Education*, *66*, 60–63.

Glasser, W. (1978). Disorders in our schools: causes and remedies. *Phi Delta Kappan*, *59*, 331–333.

Glasser, W. (1985). *Control theory in the classroom*. New York: Perennial Library.

PART TWO

From Models to Classroom Practice

CHAPTER 9

Classrooms That Reduce Misbehavior

In Chapter 8 you saw how William Glasser has changed his primary emphasis from corrective to preventive discipline. Teachers express mixed feelings about this change. Experience has taught them that no approach can prevent all misbehavior; you still have to deal with that. But they would certainly rather prevent misbehavior than use corrective discipline, so they pay serious attention to anything of a preventive nature.

Glasser proposed cooperative learning as a major solution to student misbehavior. We will learn more about that approach later in this chapter. But that's certainly not the only strategy teachers can use to reduce misbehavior. Many other strategies deserve careful attention, among them: (1) working to enhance students' self-concepts, (2) building a positive sense of purpose within the group, (3) giving attention to their personal ways of teaching, since teaching *style* (as contrasted with subject matter taught) is known to affect group performance, and (4) using effective techniques of classroom management. The last of these strategies—classroom management—is a broad topic that requires considerable explanation; it therefore is treated as a topic by itself in Chapter 10. The other four strategies—self-concept, sense of group purpose, cooperative learning, and teaching style—are examined in the remainder of this chapter.

I. ENHANCING STUDENTS' SELF-CONCEPTS

Many authorities have investigated self-concept, defined as the overall opinion that each person holds about himself or herself. Those authorities are virtually unanimous in their conclusion that a strong positive self-concept emerges as one experiences frequent success and that it is weakened by repeated failure. They further conclude that self-concept affects overall behavior, including learning. This leads to a following conclusion—that when teachers enhance students' self-concepts they simultaneously increase learning while reducing misbehavior.

Three factors play prominent roles in building student self-concept. They are: (1) regular personal attention from the teacher, (2) experiencing genuine success, and (3) recognition for that success. Let us see what teachers can do to ensure that these three factors are prominent in their classrooms.

Personal Attention from the Teacher

Most of us, when thinking back on the teachers we most admired and appreciated, realize that those teachers gave us much personal attention. They acknowledged us, spoke with us, encouraged us, pushed us, and enjoyed the improvements we made. As a result we came to see ourselves as worthwhile. We felt we belonged and that someone important cared about us. We realized that while we made mistakes we were nonetheless capable, and finally we came to believe in ourselves. (Incidentally, by helping your students believe in their own capabilities to succeed, you give them the greatest gift teachers can give!)

Encapsulated in the previous paragraph is the formula for providing positive personal attention to students. You treat them as fellow human beings. You talk with them as with friends, individually. At the same time you give them encouragement, support, and even strong pushes when necessary. You let them know in a kind way that second-rate is not good enough, that we all make many mistakes but progress only as we overcome them.

Providing Genuine Success

People can often think they are successful when they are not. This can occur when they are acknowledged or rewarded for accomplishments that are mediocre at best. Students can be told they are "really learning" or "behaving great" when in fact they are not. Teachers sometimes do this to try to keep their students in a good mood. But any sense of success that this approach engenders is false, and sooner or later the students will recognize that fact and realize that they have been short-changed.

That is why the term "genuine success" is used here. It refers to true accomplishments, to significant improvements, to tasks done well. This genuine success is available to every student in the classroom (even though it is difficult to get all students to take advantage of it). One of the teacher's main tasks is to arrange instruction so that the largest number of students do in fact experience genuine success frequently.

This task is not so difficult to perform as it might at first appear. It is accomplished by doing the following: (1) using clear goals as targets, (2) using a curriculum that progresses, (3) providing direction and urging, (4) using good instructional materials, and (5) developing esprit de corps. Let us see what is involved in each.

Clear Goals As Targets. Goals indicate what students are to accomplish. In order to be effective in promoting success they must be clearly understood by the students and must be seen as attainable.

Goals should be discussed with students, clarifying what they mean, why they are important, and how they can be reached. It is a good idea to share them with students' parents as well. This knowledge motivates students, reassures them, and helps guide their work. Timelines and progress checkpoints can be established for goals that take longer to reach, thereby helping students know whether they are progressing as expected.

Curriculum That Progresses. When students are involved in a class curriculum that leads them forward in a cumulative fashion (as opposed to hit and miss activities used for filling time), they have frequent opportunities for experiencing success. Such a curriculum is sequenced so that new learnings are built on top of prior learnings, leading from the known to the unknown. Students can easily see that they are acquiring new learnings and becoming steadily more competent. Their progress should be frequently acknowledged.

Direction and Urging. Like it or not, you the teacher are the prime motivator in the classroom. Many students are neither self-directed nor self-controlled, and they will not work well on their own for long periods of time even in the best activities. That fact puts teachers continually in a role of guiding, exhorting, entertaining, monitoring, providing feedback, and otherwise encouraging students to complete their work.

The importance of this role can hardly be overemphasized. It is more important to student success than any other factor. True, we see an occasional student who learns well without a teacher. But most of us do not have sufficient motivation to do so, nor can we learn rapidly without guidance. And let's face it—most of us need a taskmaster as well, if we are to do our best. On the positive side, teacher urging, enthusiasm, and enjoyment of student progress not only motivate students, but have an overall effect of making schooling more enjoyable for students and teachers alike.

Good Instructional Materials. Proper instructional materials enliven learning by making the subject more interesting, clearer, and more understandable. They provide extensions, examples, illustrations, problems, and entertainment. They allow students to explore further afield and permit easier application of new learnings into realistic situations.

There is no way that most of us can visit the Amazon Jungle, the Pyramids, Antarctica, or the Laplanders in Finland. There is no way we can see molecules, solar systems, or the inner workings of nuclear reactors. But students must deal with such topics in their daily learning. Instructional materials allow them to do so with much greater likelihood of understanding and success.

Esprit De Corps. Success depends in large measure on morale. Morale is closely related to the phenomenon called esprit de corps—group spirit. Esprit de corps enlivens an entire group. It provides stimulation, direction, sense of purpose, sense of value. All teachers hope for it, but few know how to bring it about.

Unfortunately, the recipe for esprit de corps does not always work. It consists of poorly defined portions of teacher enthusiasm, personal attention to students, golden-rule concern for each other among students, an enjoyable curriculum, and liberal sprinkles of success. The single indispensable ingredient, however, is the following: the class must believe it is exceptional in some important way—the highest achieving, the most considerate, the best-working, the closest-knit, whatever. Groups that acquire this feeling develop great energy. They produce more, learn more, and enjoy the learning experiences more than do other groups.

Recognition for Success

Most of us have a general idea of whether or not we are being successful in our work or studies, but we are never quite sure unless we have considerable amounts of feedback from others. Just as our self-concept grows from the basis of what we believe others think of us, so does our sense of success. For that reason it is important that teachers take pains to ensure not only that student success occur, but that it be recognized by others as well. The following are suggestions on how to provide recognition for success.

Chart Group Gains. Gains and other improvements shown by the class as a whole can be shown by means of graphs, time lines, class diaries, and sometimes by class murals. Students can make these charts and graphs, which should be colorful and attractive, and post them in the classroom.

Many elementary classes prepare timelines, made of string or paper and placed high along the walls, to show progress. Others make murals that illustrate activities and accomplishments. These are popular for display at open houses and other school events attended by parents. Elementary and secondary classes can keep class diaries, with students taking turns in making entries decided on by the class. This provides a documented history of class activities and accomplishments, which students very much enjoy reading later in the year.

Chart Personal Gains. Charts showing individual progress are very motivating for students. Such charts may not be displayed in the classroom if they show any students in a derogatory light, but all students may keep them in personal folders shared by the teacher. Such charts can indicate the student's reaching objectives, amount of work attempted, amount of work completed, percentage of correct responses, and so forth. Parents also react very well to such documentation of the child's performance. This helps cast teachers in a favorable light because it indicates the teacher's specific plans and efforts to help the student succeed.

Inform Parents. Parents should be regularly informed about the success (not just the lack thereof) experienced by their child in school. This information can easily be provided through student reports to parents, teacher communication with parents, and materials that show student progress in class.

Students need to be instructed on how to report success to parents. Periodically, as at the end of the day for elementary students and the end of the week for secondary students, teachers should take a few minutes to review with students what they have accomplished. They are then encouraged to relay this information to their parents.

Systematic communication from teacher to parents is also excellent for publicizing group and individual success. It does take some time, but it pays good dividends. Teachers can send notes home with students, send weekly newsletters, and make very brief telephone calls. In all cases, the purpose is to convey accomplishment and success, not to speak of problems. (Of course problems must be dealt with too, but in separate communications.)

Parents are very eager to see samples of their child's work. Worksheets, assignments, and test results can be shared with parents. Teachers must be very careful, though, that work they send home has been checked correctly. Any errors made by the teacher are almost certain to be noticed by parents, and one tiny mistake can undo the good that may have taken weeks to build.

Share In The Classroom. Students need to receive attention from their peers, to have their classmates recognize their efforts and their accomplishments. They can get this attention through oral presentations, demonstrations, displays of work, and bringing into the classroom some of their own handiwork. Many students will be shy and reluctant to participate. They should be encouraged as much as possible, but not forced if they are terrified.

Often the work of the class can be shared publicly. Fairly common are class plays and other programs, science fairs, arts and crafts fairs, and so forth. Students are highly motivated to do quality work when they know it is to be displayed publicly. Those who are invited to the performances or displays add greatly to a student's sense of success as they acknowledge student efforts and talk with students individually about their work.

Produce A Class Newsletter. Most classes can produce a class newsletter on a monthly or quarterly basis. This newsletter can explain what is going on in the class, contain samples of student work, present announcements of displays and performances, and include anything else the class desires. To be most effective, its tone should be businesslike (not silly or gossipy) and it should include all the students' names in one place or another.

The newsletter is delivered to parents, administrators, and others, even at times to a few community organizations and businesses. Local newspapers usually take an interest in them. Few avenues can so well publicize the efforts and achievements of students. The positive attention they bring from parents and community does much for the self-esteem of students, teachers, and school personnel.

II. BUILDING A POSITIVE SENSE OF GROUP PURPOSE

In the first model of discipline presented in this book, Redl and Wattenberg pointed out that people in groups behave differently than they do individually. Groups seem to take on an identity and personality of their own, but unlike individuals' personalities, which are fairly consistent over time, group personalities are quite prone to change, in accord with certain influences (technically called "group dynamics") that routinely play upon them.

It goes without saying that teachers want their classes to be energetic, hard-working, courteous, and joyful. It also goes without saying, unfortunately, that only an occasional class shows these desired traits. Teachers know that problem students (rotten apples) can spoil the personality of a class, but most teachers do not fully recognize—or at least do not know how to control—the influences that produce the positive class personalities they desire.

Let us see, then, what teachers can do in order to bring about the sort of positive sense of purpose and enjoyment that they would like to see in their classes.

A Sense of Togetherness

A first step for teachers at the beginning of the year or semester is to work toward developing the sense that the class is a unit that lives and works together, that all members are striving toward a common goal, that all face a common set of obstacles, that all benefit from helping each other, that all lose something when any member is unsuccessful, and that all can take justifiable pride in the accomplishments of the class.

Contrast that group view with the individualistic view, where students who manage to be successful are prized and rewarded but the unsuccessful are frequently slighted by the teacher and disparaged by the group. The unsuccessful students then begin to behave in one of two ways: most of them give up and stop participating (which produces only an uncomfortable partial sense of failure for the teacher), while a few of them become actively disruptive and nonconforming to class rules—the rotten apples that spoil the entire classroom barrel.

It should be acknowledged that the rotten apples are not always the nonachievers. Some highly achieving, highly competitive students develop an arrogantly superior attitude where they hog the spotlight and sarcastically put down the contributions of others. This kind of behavior does even more to destroy the sense of classroom camaraderie than does the balkiness of the disenchanted.

At first blush, many people do not like the notion of a highly cooperative class. It seems somehow un-American to work for the good of the group rather than for the individual. But a deeper analysis reveals that a posture of cooperation works to the benefit of all. This is so for several reasons. Most psychologists agree that a primary motive in human behavior is to gain a sense of belonging, which almost all students can achieve in a cohesive group but which some are certain not to find in a divisive group. It is also widely acknowledged that if people wish to gain the esteem of others, they can best do so by helping others build themselves, not by selfishly working at their expense. As for the fear that achievement among the most capable students declines when they help their less-capable classmates, research simply does not bear this out. As they give help to others, the achievement of capable students often rises higher than it would otherwise have been, perhaps attesting to the adage that if you want to learn something well, teach it to another.

To foster a sense of togetherness, the teacher should continually talk with the class about what they will accomplish *as a group*, how they will deal with the problems they encounter as a group, how they will work together to get the best achievement possible for every individual in the group. In order to bring this about, responsibilities are given and shared, students are encouraged to speak of their concerns while the class attempts to find remedies, and the teacher takes special steps, when necessary, to incorporate every student into the ongoing work of the class.

Purpose in Class Activities

Sense of purpose grows with student understanding of what they are expected to accomplish and how they are expected to do so. Specific short-range goals serve better than do vague long-range goals. That is, short-range goals such as completing a class mural by Friday, having every student get at least 90% correct on next week's vocabulary test, or even getting the six math problems completed by the end of the class period are much preferable to long-range goals such as (later) enjoying life more, making a better living, or passing the final test at the end of the year.

It should be noted that a sense of purposefulness is not dependent on the activities' being fun or creative. Rather, over time it is dependent on students'—at least those beyond primary grades—having a fairly good idea of the reasons behind what they are asked to do. Students come to resent busy work, and after a while they learn to spot it instantly.

Group Achievement

Traditionally, schools have focused more on individual achievement than on group achievement, as evidenced by tests and grading systems that divide students into higher and lower categories. Assumptions that appear to underly this focus were that individuals would (and should) achieve in accord with their abilities and efforts, that the main purpose of schooling was to promote individual excellence, and that there were simply many individuals who did not have the capabilities needed for school achievement.

That view has begun to change. It is now recognized that higher achievement by all members of the class (or society) benefits the class (or society) as a whole, that the less-capable students are able to accomplish more work of higher quality than previously believed, and that attitudes among all students, high and low alike, improve as they have successful experiences in dealing with challenging situations (Squires, Huitt, & Segars, 1983).

For those reasons, it is important for teachers to organize learning activities so that they lead to group, rather than individualistic, achievement. The quality of the magazine produced by the English class is made dependent on the quality of the contributions by every member of the class. The work of the math class is evaluated in terms of what the class as a whole has been able to achieve. The school principal is asked to make a special observation of Ms. Smith's class at the school assembly and provide written comments about their behavior. Every student is given a responsible role in producing the holiday performance to which the parents are invited.

Public Recognition

The sense of purposeful group behavior is greatly increased through public recognition. Teachers who recognize this fact try to find ways to draw attention to the class's accomplishments. The kindergarten class puts on its annual Thanksgiving feast, to which parents are invited. The children wear paper costumes they have helped make and display artwork and sing songs about Thanksgiving. The sixth grade holds its semiannual science fair, which features science projects that students have worked on together. The physical education department presents its recreational sports night for the invited public, with entire classes demonstrating rhythmic exercises and collaborative "new games." The graphics arts class presents its annual multimedia display in a city shopping mall, with large photographs of the students working on their projects.

Events such as these are often reported in the local newspapers and occasionally on television. When students work on projects such as these and receive public recognition for what they have done, their sense of purposeful, responsible behavior improves dramatically, with a corresponding reduction in apathetic and disruptive behavior.

III. COOPERATIVE LEARNING AND ITS EFFECTS ON DISCIPLINE

In the previous discussions concerning the importance of developing purposeful, cohesive classes, you saw many references to cooperation, mutual support, and group achievement. You no doubt recognized the relationship between that sense of group learning and what is called "cooperative learning," as advocated by Nevin (1984), Glasser (1985), Johnson, Johnson, Holubec, and Roy (1984), and Parker (1985).

As you saw in Chapter 8, William Glasser maintains that if educational programs (not to mention discipline systems) are to be effective, certain student needs must be met, specifically the needs for belonging, for power, for freedom, and for having fun.

Glasser and others believe that at present *cooperative learning* is the instructional strategy best able to provide for these four needs. Not only does cooperative learning meet student needs for belonging (as a valued member of the group), for fun (through talking and working with others), and for a bit of freedom (in making decisions), but it provides what Glasser contends is the most important need of all for secondary students—power. Glasser says that few people recognize the centrality of the power need among secondary students, a need that is normally met only in physical education, athletics, drama, and musical performing groups. This power need consists partly of power to influence other people, but in large part it is power to do something well and be recognized for it.

In supporting his conclusions concerning cooperative learning, Glasser relied heavily on the works of David Johnson et al. presented in their book, *Circles of Learning: Cooperation in the Classroom* (1984). The observations and suggestions presented in the following pages of this chapter are derived from that book and from Glasser's book *Control Theory in the Classroom* (1985).

What Is Cooperative Learning?

Cooperative learning is described as small groups of students working together to complete instructional activities. Groups are comprised of no fewer than two members and no more than six. Four students per group is favored by most teachers who use cooperative learning. But simply sitting together and talking does not constitute cooperative learning. According to Johnson et al. (1984, p. 8), the following four elements are necessary for cooperative learning:

1. *Positive interdependence.* This distinction is crucial: the students must be dependent on each other in the completion of the activities. This dependency can be accomplished by assigning students to different roles within the group; the overall task connot be completed without the contributions of each member.
2. *Face-to-face interaction.* Students must be able to interact and exchange information easily.
3. *Individual accountability.* The learning teams help maximize learning for each member, and each member is held individually accountable for accomplishing the intended learnings. Students comprising the groups have different ability and achievement levels; they are usually assigned so as to provide a mix of abilities. This allows

TABLE 9.1. A COMPARISON OF COOPERATIVE AND TRADITIONAL LEARNING

Cooperative Learning	Traditional Learning
Much collaboration	Little collaboration
Much interdependence	Little interdependence
Individual accountability	Individual accountability
Heterogeneous	Homogeneous or heterogeneous
Shared leadership	Undefined leadership
Shared responsibility	Responsibility for self
Social skills directly taught	Social skills usually assumed
Groups analyze effectiveness	Little analysis of effectiveness

students to learn from each other while providing mutual assistance and support.

4. *Use of interpersonal and small-group skills.* Students must use the social skills necessary for collaborative learning, but often such skills are lacking. Therefore, students must be taught how to use such skills as leadership, effective communication, and conflict management. In their groups they are given time and procedures for analyzing the overall effectiveness of their group work.

The differences between this cooperative learning approach and traditional classroom learning is summarized in Table 9.1.

Is Cooperative Learning Any Good?

Both Glasser and Johnson et al. contend that society and education are beset with many ills that can be addressed through cooperative learning. The main societal ill, they assert, is the competitive outlook that: (1) causes individuals to attempt to excel *at the expense* of their peers, and (2) provides ultimate success for only a small number of individuals, while the majority lag behind, lose interest, and become unproductive. This competitive, individualistic stance does not adequately prepare students for cooperative efforts required of them in later work and home lives (Johnson et al., p. 10).

The main educational ill is that traditional classroom practices do not meet students' basic needs adequately to cause them to consider the work worthwhile. That is, at least half of the students, by the time they reach high school, consider their classes neither fun nor helpful, nor are their needs for belonging and freedom met in such classes.

These are bold contentions. Do they have any basis in fact? Johnson et al. analyzed 122 studies into how school achievement is affected when interdependence (cooperation) is stressed in learning. They found that:

...cooperative learning experiences tend to promote higher achievement than do competitive and individualistic learning experiences. These results hold for all age levels, for all subject areas, and for tasks involving concept attainment, verbal problem solving, categorization, spatial problem solving, retention and memory, motor performance, and guessing-judging-predicting. For rote-decoding and correcting tasks, cooperation seems to be equally effective as competitive and individualistic learning procedures (p. 15).

They also concluded from their analysis of the research that:

1. There is no type of learning for which cooperation is *less* effective than traditional teaching.
2. The discussion process in cooperative learning promotes the development of higher cognitive skills.
3. Cooperative learning promotes peer regulation, feedback, and encouragement, which are seldom seen in individualistic learning.
4. Motivation to learn seems to increase in cooperative learning groups.
5. Cooperative learning promotes more positive attitudes toward the subject and the learning activities.
6. Cooperative learning seems to produce better social relations, stronger personal identity, and increased optimism and trust in other people.
7. Cooperative learning seems to result in students viewing the teacher as more supportive and accepting.

How Is Cooperative Learning Done in the Classroom?

Johnson et al. provide a number of detailed suggestions for forming co-operative learning groups and helping them work most effectively. The following are some of their suggestions:

1. *Assigning students to groups.* Group size depends on the maturity of students and their ability to interact. Groups should be small enough so that everyone will engage in the discussions. Three to five students is about right in most cases (many teachers favor groups of four). Groups should contain both high and low achieving students, and should be assigned by the teacher rather than selected by students.
2. *Changing the groups.* Groups should remain together long enough for them to be productive. Those that have difficulties can profit from working out their differences. By changing groups every

month or two, it is possible to cause most of the class members to work closely together during the semester or year.

3. *Arranging the seating.* Johnson et al. advise teachers to arrange the groups in small circles so that eye contact and easy exchange are enhanced. But in most classrooms, rectangular tables or desks are standard furniture, making it difficult to seat students in small circles. In practice, most teachers seat the students in rectangles or squares.

4. *Assigning roles.* Each group member is assigned a specific role so as to ensure interdependence. Examples of roles are: *summarizer-checker*, who makes sure everyone understands what is being learned; *encourager*, who reinforces members' contributions; *recorder*, who writes down the group's decisions and accomplishments; and a *researcher-runner*, who obtains needed materials, looks up information, and so on.

5. *Explaining the academic task.* Make sure students understand what they are supposed to do, how they are to do it, and what they are to accomplish in the end. Emphasize that they must work collaboratively and that all of them are responsible for learning the assigned material. If they produce a single paper, report, or other product, each is to sign that they agree with its contents.

6. *Monitoring and providing assistance.* Teachers should circulate and carefully monitor the work of each group, noting whether procedures are being followed correctly. However, they should not answer student questions about the work or procedures unless the entire group is uncertain. Students should obtain such information from each other when possible.

7. *Closing the lessons.* To end the lessons, students should summarize what they have learned, accomplished, produced, and so forth. They may also be asked to evaluate how well their group worked together.

8. *Evaluating group work.* Work done by the total group is judged on its own merits (criterion-referenced) rather than compared to the work of other groups. Tests of achievement may be given, with individual students accountable for their own learning. Teachers may wish to assign one grade for the work accomplished and a second for how well the group worked together.

These basic suggestions are put into actual practice in a number of modified ways. In *Control Theory in the Classroom*, William Glasser presents several descriptive episodes recounting real teachers' use of cooperative learning. (Glasser, by the way, uses the term "learning teams," since he has found that many parents do not like the term "cooperative learning.")

Glasser's real-life scenarios exemplify the personal modifications that most teachers make when using cooperative learning in their classrooms.

Comment On Cooperative Learning

Despite the well-documented advantages of cooperative learning, it would defy common sense to conclude that all learning occurs best through the cooperative mode. Quite the opposite is true. Much learning is done individually; many people prefer to learn that way. It is difficult to believe that many students would prefer reading favorite books, or delving into special interests, or producing creative products in collaboration with others who do not share their interests or talents. And it would be a mistake to remove the stimulation of occasional competition. Learning is often made much more exciting by adding competition, at least briefly. Can you imagine learning to debate, or play football, or enter science fairs without the competitive urge to outdo your peers?

As for cooperative work being best for *all* students in a group, one must question whether the most capable individuals benefit from working together on academic tasks with the least able students. They may, in fact, be hindered by students who are progressing at much slower rates. And as for all students being motivated, the reality is that groups are sometimes going to contain nonworking members who hamper the efforts of the other students while taking credit for work they did not do.

Despite these concerns about cooperative learning, the advantages it affords are impressive. Teachers who have used it in their classrooms usually become advocates, although they use it only in certain subjects and activities. They report that most, but not all, of their students like it. In conclusion, Glasser is probably correct in his strong advocacy of learning teams in the classroom. Such teams probably do meet student needs for belonging, power, fun, and freedom, while providing the bonus of higher achievement and better attitudes among the majority of students.

IV. TEACHER STYLES AND THEIR EFFECTS ON STUDENTS

We would be remiss if we did not acknowledge the effects that different teaching styles have on students. While there is no one type of teacher personality that is best for producing learning, there does seem to be a general way of teaching—in other words, a style of teaching—that produces overall best results in both classroom learning and control of misbehavior. Fortunately, it is within all teachers' ability to develop an effective style of teaching, as we will see.

Types of Teachers

Not all teachers are able to maintain good discipline in their classrooms. Where there is poor discipline, students tend to learn less, have little respect for their teacher, and show poorer attitude toward school. On the other hand, many teachers maintain very good classroom discipline. It is no surprise to find that their students usually learn more, have greater respect for the teacher, and show a more positive attitude toward school.

It is on these teachers with better discipline that we now focus. They may be of three fairly distinct types, that we will call *well-liked teachers, efficient teachers*, and *master teachers*. Keep in mind that the three types are not mutually exclusive. Not only is there overlap among the types, but some teachers waver from day to day, especially as regards efficiency.

The *well-liked* teacher is enjoyed and supported by the students. They like to be in these teachers' classrooms. Good academic learning can occur in well-liked teachers' classrooms, but often learning is only mediocre and sometimes it is poor. Students behave well because they like and want to please the teacher, and they want the teacher to like them in return.

The *efficient* teacher is one who plans, organizes, teaches, and manages well. Everything goes like clockwork; nothing is left to chance. Achievement tends to be high in their classrooms. But teachers can be very efficient without being particularly stimulating or caring. Efficient teachers are not, therefore, always well liked. Students respect them and may grudgingly express gratitude and admiration, but since they are often uncomfortable in classrooms where there is little personal warmth, they do not enjoy the educational experience. Students behave well not so much because they are internally motivated to do so, but because, first, they have little opportunity to misbehave in the tightly structured program and, second, because efficient teachers have structured systems of rules and consequences that they are able to invoke consistently.

Master teachers display the qualities that epitomize the best in teaching. They are efficient, yet flexible. They show that they care about their students. In addition, they do what they can to make learning interesting, exciting, and satisfying. Their students learn well, admire and respect them, and usually like them personally. Good behavior occurs because of the teacher's reasonable standards and personal concern for the students. The students, in turn, behave well because they want to please the teacher. As time goes on, they tend to value good behavior as a proper end in itself.

How To Be a Well-Liked Teacher

In 1936, Hart conducted a study in which he asked a number of students to list the traits they liked best in their teachers. Prominent among the traits identified were friendliness, flexibility, and sense of humor. Student preference for those traits has held steady over the half-century since Hart's study, as shown by Mosley and Smith (1982) who asked over 500 secondary students the question "What do you like about the ways teachers help you learn?" The students replied that they liked their teachers to joke and make learning fun, give individual attention to students, make the subject interesting, make expectations clear, and maintain a positive, relaxed learning atmosphere.

How to Be an Efficient Teacher

What students like in their teachers and what seems best to help them learn subject matter do not seem to be strongly related. In fact, it is often observed that some teachers who consistently produce high student learning are not particularly warm, friendly, or humorous. Their effectiveness is due to something else, justifying the conclusion that there is no specific set of personality traits that ensures teacher effectiveness (Wlodkowski, 1977).

But if not personality, then what causes the difference among teachers? Research during the past decade has brought to light several teacher behaviors that produce higher academic learning. All together, the behaviors characterize what is herein called the efficient teacher. Greenblatt, Cooper, and Muth (1984) compiled a list of the characteristics identified through research. Included within their list were the following:

The teacher:

1. Is clear and businesslike.
2. Keeps students on task.
3. Provides positive corrective feedback.
4. Structures the lessons.
5. Manages instruction to keep it free from disruptions.
6. Paces lessons in accord with student ability and interest.

Teachers who do these things usually produce higher than average academic achievement among their students. The students may or may not like the teacher, however.

How to Be a Master Teacher

We have used the term master teacher to refer to teachers who produce high achievement and who at the same time are respected, admired, and liked by their students. These are the teachers who are likely to have the greatest impact on students' personal growth in self-concept and self-confidence, with resultant effects that are long lasting.

Master teachers organize well, but they are not slaves to the organization. They remain flexible in accord with the circumstances. They provide stimulating lessons, but they remember that the lessons are for the students and that, in fact, the students must always remain the primary concern of the educational process. When you see such teachers, they are likely to display the following characteristics:

1. They provide worthwhile, stimulating learning experiences.
2. They give personal attention regularly to every student.
3. They maintain a warm, helpful, positive class atmosphere.
4. They provide careful guidance and feedback.
5. They often teach with a certain flair.
6. They manage class activities and routines well.

Another way to describe the master teacher is to consider what they do with regard to learning experiences, facilitation, and management. The *learning experiences* they provide are attractive and well organized. They meet students' personal and academic needs. The experiences tend to be stimulating, often with an air of adventure and mystery. Students are usually actively involved, rather than passive, in the experiences.

Master teachers *facilitate* learning by providing appropriate structure, guidance, help, and feedback. They are well organized. They explain clearly what students are to do. They present lessons well. They guide students to complete work on their own, but are careful not to be too directive or constrictive. They vary their teaching methods and make good application of effective motivational and communicative techniques.

With regard to *management*, master teachers are adept at keeping their classes flowing smoothly, without interruptions or other awkward breaks. They establish standards for work and behavior. They involve the students in setting those standards, so as to develop a sense of ownership among students, and they refer back to the standards as often as necessary. When they must deal unpleasantly with students, they take care to focus on the behavior they expect rather than on shortcomings in the students. They are firmly assertive, but fair.

Application Exercises

1. Think back on your own experiences as a student. Did you have a teacher who had a positive influence on your self-concept? What specifically did that teacher do that improved your estimation of yourself?
2. Suppose you are teaching either creative writing or vocal music.

Explain specifically how you would discuss the goals with students so they would understand: (a) what they were supposed to accomplish, (b) why the learnings were important, and (c) what they could do to show they had reached the goal.

3. Explain how group gains could be charted for classes in spelling, American history, and algebra.

4. Select a grade level or subject you are most interested in teaching. Suppose you decided to produce a class newsletter. What would you have it include? What roles and responsibilities would you have the students assume? Overall, do you think the results would justify the efforts and time spent on it?

5. Assess the value of cooperative learning versus traditional teaching in the following topics: swimming; spelling; oil painting; multiplication drills; New England geography; classical Greek architecture; a simulated voyage up the Amazon.

6. For the subject or grade you prefer teaching, to what extent do you think you could use learning teams? For what would they be appropriate? Inappropriate?

7. Suppose you were using learning teams in your classroom and a parent complained that she didn't want her son to have to waste time helping slower students. What could you say that would explain your position while at the same time reassuring her about her son?

8. Assess yourself at the present time concerning whether you would most closely resemble a well-liked teacher, an efficient teacher, or a master teacher. Be specific about your strengths and deficiencies. What might you do to further strengthen your abilities?

REFERENCES

Glasser, W. (1985). *Control theory in the classroom.* New York: Perennial Library.

Greenblatt, R., Cooper, B., & Muth, R. (1984). Managing for effective teaching. *Educational Leadership, 41*, 57–59, February.

Hart, J. (1936). *Teachers and teaching.* New York: Macmillan.

Johnson, D., Johnson, R., Holubec, E., & Roy, P. (1984). *Circles of learning: cooperation in the classroom.* Alexandria, VA: Association for Supervision and Curriculum Development.

Mosley, M., & Smith, P. (1982). What works in learning? Students provide the answers. *Phi Delta Kappan, 64*, 273.

Parker, R. (1985). Small group cooperative learning. *Education Digest, 51*, 44–46.

Squires, D., Huitt, W., & Segars, J. (1983). *Effective schools and classrooms: a research-based perspective.* Alexandria, VA: Association for Supervision and Curriculum Development.

Wlodkowski, R. (1977). *Motivation.* Washington, D.C.: The National Education Association.

CHAPTER 10

Classroom Management for Preventive Discipline

The techniques you have learned so far should enable you to deal with virtually all types of misbehavior that you are likely to encounter in the classroom—even (if you use the techniques appropriately) in those urban classrooms in which misbehavior is the rule rather than the exception. Even when you are able to deal with misbehavior effectively, however, you will find that discipline situations produce stress and dampen everyone's enthusiasm for school. They slow down the learning process, cause tension in both teacher and students and occasionally influence your feelings toward particular students. For these reasons, anything that you can do to prevent misbehavior yields a bonus of enjoyment and enthusiasm for the entire classroom.

Effective classroom management is very powerful in preventing misbehavior. Classroom management refers to how you *organize, deliver, monitor,* and *communicate* your instructional program. It includes attention to the myriad details of routines and how you treat and interact with your students (Fifer, 1986). When management is poor, the class is in constant turmoil. Students act as though they don't remember what to do or how or when to do it. Nonproductive noise is high. Nerves become ragged. Students are dissatisfied. Misbehavior increases. Your own stress level rises, and teaching becomes more and more distasteful.

With good classroom management, however, a completely different picture prevails. The curriculum flows smoothly, with relatively few prob-

153

lems. Most of your attention goes to helping students learn (Brophy, 1985). Your students enjoy the class, and you feel successful and rewarded.

This chapter does not deal with misbehavior *per se*, but rather with aspects of management that are known to *reduce the incidence* of misbehavior. The management aspects considered here are *classroom climate, routines, and communication*.

MANAGING THE CLASSROOM CLIMATE

The Meaning of Climate

Climate refers to the *feeling tone* that prevails in the classroom. This feeling tone is a composite of attitudes, emotions, values, and relationships. While it is vaguely defined, all teachers are keenly aware of its existence, and they can almost always tell when it is good or bad. Climate probably has as much to do with learning, productive work, and self-concept as does anything else in the educational program.

A poor classroom climate is characterized as either chaotic and disorganized or cold, unfriendly, and threatening. Such climates discourage learning, although threatening environments may cause students to work under duress (which then makes them dislike both teacher and school). If coldly and rigidly controlled, students fear to make errors. They obey the rules so the teacher will not take reprisals against them. A general lack of humor prevails, replaced by sarcasm and animosity.

In contrast, a good classroom climate is characterized as warm, supportive, and pleasant. It is friendly and filled with good nature and acceptance; it is encouraging and helpful, with low levels of threat. All together, such a climate encourages productive work and promotes a sense of enjoyment and accomplishment for everyone.

> Cynthia, an elementary teacher, describes how she attempts to set the tone in her classroom (Charles, 1983):
> "I begin the year with a discussion about my expectations for the year. I tell the children that I consider them my 'school family.' I explain that just as in any family we might not always agree on everything, but that I will always care about them. I say that each and every one of them is very special and important to me, and that I want them to have the best possible school year. Because they are so important to me, I will not tolerate any cruelty or unkindness to each other. I expect them to be the best behaved and well-mannered class in the entire school, both in the classroom and on the playground. I tell them that good behavior is really just good manners, because it shows respect for others, whether children or adults. I also go over the golden rule, and I make a bulletin board on that theme. I refer to the golden rule as our class

motto. That is the only rule we have in the class, and I discuss with them how it covers everything. If you don't want to be called names, then don't call other people names. If you want people to listen to you, then be sure to listen to others. And most important, if you want to have friends, then be a friend. The children seem to understand and accept all of this very well. They see it as a fair and sensible way to do things, and I think it helps them know they have a teacher who cares about them.''

Human Relations Skills and Classroom Climate

Learning to manage the classroom climate calls for attention to human relations skills. These skills have to do with the improvement of interactions among individuals in the classroom. Three focuses of human relations skills should be understood and implemented: *general human relations skills; human relations between teacher and students; and human relations skills between teacher and parents.*

General Human Relations Skills. Four general skills of human relations are valuable to almost everyone in all situations. They are friendliness, positive attitude, ability to listen, and ability to compliment genuinely.

Friendliness is a trait everyone admires, yet many of us have difficulty in showing it toward others, especially when threatened or with people we dislike. Yet we can behave in friendly ways even with people who displease us by smiling, speaking gently, calling the other person by name, asking how they are, asking about their family and work, and so on. When we behave in this way, we find that others begin to respond similarly. Purposeful small talk can be a useful asset.

A *positive attitude* means that we focus on the brighter side of things. When dealing with problems we look for solutions rather than lamenting obstacles or blaming others. We refrain from complaining, backbiting, and malicious gossip. When we speak positively, others begin to do so as well.

Ability to listen is a trait we admire in others, but often find lacking in ourselves. It seems most of us would rather express our minds than listen to what others have to say. Yet, listening produces so many desirable outcomes that it behooves teachers to cultivate the habit. Listening shows that we take a genuine interest in the other person, an essential first step in paving the way to positive relationships. It shows that we value the other person's opinions, especially if we learn to reflect their comments back to them without expressing our value judgments. Finally, it improves the quality of communication by permitting a true exchange of ideas.

Ability to *compliment genuinely* is a behavior that receives relatively little attention in human relations but is nonetheless a factor of considerable power. Many of us are unable to compliment others, for fear of appearing insincere. We have seen how some people use compliments falsely in hopes of currying favor. Nevertheless, it is obvious that we like to receive compliments, even when unable to receive them gracefully. You can check yourself on this by reflecting on your attitude toward people who compliment you as compared to people who do not (or who give you unsolicited "constructive criticism"). With which of the two would you rather work and socialize?

As you learn to give compliments, however, you must make sure they are genuine and that the other person sees them as such. It helps if you make your compliment explicit: rather than saying "Your ideas are brilliant," you might say "Your explanation of the Persian viewpoint is the most understandable I have heard." On a more personal level, rather than saying "Hey, looking great today!" you might say "That color surely suits you."

Human Relations With Students. The general skills of human relations apply to everyone in all situations. When working with students, however, there are additional relations skills that teachers should employ. They are *giving regular attention, using reinforcement, showing continual willingness to help, and modeling courtesy and good manners.*

Giving regular attention to students does much to build bonds of trust and cooperation. You can give this attention in several different ways. One way is to speak frequently, but briefly, with individual students, often about topics other than school work. You should spread your attention around to all students. It has been documented that teachers give most of their attention to two small groups of students: the higher-achieving and those who are behavior problems. This leaves a large segment of the class who receive little personal attention. You should make a special point of speaking with such students when they enter or exit the room, while you monitor their work, and when you encounter them outside the classroom. Your personal attention contributes greatly to their sense of belonging and to their feeling that you are interested in them.

Reinforcement, as you know, is the supplying of "rewards" for student behavior, resulting in the likelihood that the behavior will be repeated or strengthened. In the realm of human relations, these reinforcements are given verbally and behaviorally, to show support, encouragement, understanding, and approval, with the result that student attention and work output increase. Examples of verbal reinforcers are: "You are showing improvement in your handwriting every day." "I can see you put a great deal of thought into preparing your essay." "Thanks a lot for being so helpful today." Examples of behavioral reinforcers are nods, smiles, winks, thumbs-up, and other expressions and gestures that show approval.

Continual willingness to help is a trait much admired in teachers.

Students gravitate to helpful teachers, tend to admire them, and usually remember them years later as quite significant. You hear them say, as adults, "Yeah, Miss Smith was strict, but she really tried to help every one of us."

Modeling courtesy and good manners is extremely effective in establishing and maintaining a positive classroom climate. You should make it a point to demonstrate in your own behavior the best of what you would like to see in your students. Even when they are boorish, you should be genteel. When they forget their manners you should make it clear that you remember yours. As mentioned before, this sort of behavior is catching. If you want your students to live by the golden rule, you yourself must be a prime example of what it means when put into practice.

Human Relations With Parents. Teachers have a responsibility to communicate with the parents of the students they teach. Many teachers accept this responsibility and use it to their advantage. Others avoid it, feeling that parents don't care and don't want to be bothered, or else that communicating with parents is more trouble than it is worth. Yet there is little doubt that in most cases teachers who communicate with parents can count on increased parental support.

The general skills of human relations described earlier apply here. In addition, for building stronger relationships with parents teachers should *communicate regularly, communicate clearly, describe expectations clearly, and emphasize the child's progress while playing down the child's shortcomings.*

Teachers are well advised to *communicate regularly* with parents. This can be done through notes, telephone calls, and newsletters. If you are able to make this effort, you show that you are interested in the welfare of the student. You also show respect for the parent as a concerned party to the student's education. This causes parents to think highly of you and to support you and the school.

This regular communication should be done very clearly. Remember that most parents do not understand educational jargon such as "critical thinking" or "cognitive levels," nor do they recognize acronyms such as SAT, IEP, or GATE. It is also wise to avoid involved sentence structure and the use of big words where little ones suffice. In short, make sure the messages you convey to parents are clear, simple, and to the point.

In communicating with parents, *clearly describe the expectations you have for their child.* Most parents like to know something about the program you are making available to their child, together with what the child is expected to do. They like to know how the child will be evaluated. They especially like to know what is expected concerning homework and their role in it, if any.

When you communicate to parents about their child, always remember one thing: no parent likes to hear his or her child criticized. Criticism is a sure way to shut off most parents at once, for they see shortcomings in their child as being shortcomings in themselves. Therefore, you must be sure to *emphasize the child's progress* while *downplaying the child's shortcomings.*

This is a matter of emphasis, not of honesty and dishonesty. If you have to communicate with a parent about a student who is having problems or presenting difficulties in school, you do not pretend nothing at all is wrong. You simply proceed tactfully, following a sequence such as this:

1. Comment on something positive about the child.
2. Mention or show progress that is being made.
3. Allude to your plans for the child that will result in still further progress.
4. Now mention difficulties that are interfering with the child's attainment of future goals, but assure the parent that you have a plan for overcoming the difficulties and that you need the parent's support in working for the well-being of the child.

It is unrealistic to think that this gentle approach will leave parents feeling great, but it will usually help them understand the situation and bring them to your support, rather than turn them against you.

Managing Classroom Routines

Keith, a secondary math teacher, describes how he works toward efficiency:

"It is important to me for things to run smoothly. I begin the period with a one-minute timed exercise. The students know I will quickly say 'go,' and if they don't have their pencils, scratch paper, and test sheet ready they are out of luck—they can try again the next day.

The subject matter is very important to me. Assignments are to be completed. If they are not, a note goes home, filled out by the student, stating what was not completed and why. The work must be made up on their own time. I go over all the assignments ahead of time so students know exactly what is expected. They know the schedule of tests and what they have to do to earn their grades. This makes them responsible for their own grades. Occasionally I receive a call from a parent whose child has received a failing grade for the first time ever. Their anger quickly subsides when I remind them that the child knew exactly what work was required for a good grade, and I explain how little the child did.

This may sound harsh, but I treat the students with great respect and courtesy. I always say 'please' and 'thank you' and 'excuse me.' I admit my mistakes and tell the students I am sorry. They reflect my example. We are courteous, we are considerate, we have an enjoyable time, and best of all we get our work done."

Routines, the commonplace procedures and chores involved in the day-to-day classroom activities, are far more important to good discipline than most people imagine. Well-managed routines permit students to know exactly what they are supposed to do, thus cutting down on wasted time and confusion, both of which interfere with learning and tend to foster misbehavior. Teachers should, therefore, spend the time necessary for establishing routines to the point that they become habitual for the students.

Routines that require special attention include *opening and closing activities, materials usage, what to do with completed work, the use of student assistants,* and *how to provide assistance to students at work.* Suggestions for establishing these routines are given in the paragraphs that follow.

Opening And Closing Activities. In many classrooms the students waste several minutes before getting started on their work. They come into the classroom talking, are slow to take their seats, continue talking once seated, and do not begin work until the teacher's insistent voice is heard above the noise. This wasted time has a detrimental effect on both learning and student attitude toward the importance of the class.

This situation is resolved by establishing routine procedures that the students must follow when entering the room. Generally, it is best to have the students begin work immediately. This can be established as one of the class rules relating to discipline. Many different approaches are effective for beginning the class. Secondary teachers may write an assignment on the board. Students must enter, sit down, and begin work within 1 minute after the bell. Noncompliance automatically brings the negative consequences associated with the rule. Elementary teachers often have students write in journals, read silently from library books, or do math or vocabulary exercises while roll is taken. Very young children may begin by playing quietly with instructional toys or sitting quietly while the teacher or aide reads a story. In any case, the objective is to cause students to begin school activities at once, rather than talking and fooling around.

It is also important to have routines for ending activities. For classes such as art, shop, and physical education, a cleanup time is required. Students should be trained to follow established procedures within the few minutes allotted to ending the period. Other classes also benefit from routines for completing work and getting ready for dismissal.

Materials Usage. Inefficient classrooms waste time while students obtain materials and replace them after use. Procedures should be established that allow students to obtain or receive needed materials very quickly. If materials are to be distributed, several students should help, each obtaining and distributing materials to five or six other students. If students are to obtain their own materials, they should be able to go to convenient shelves or cupboards without crowding or waiting in line. Pencil sharpening can be especially distracting. Many teachers permit pencil sharpening only before class begins. Others keep containers of sharpened pencils; students can exchange their dull pencil for a sharp one when necessary.

At the end of the period the materials should be replaced as efficiently at they were obtained. Students are taught exactly what to do and are allowed a minimum of time to replace the materials.

What To Do With Completed Work. Clear procedures should be established concerning what students are to do with work they have completed. If students are allowed to come individually to the teacher and hand in their work, there is likelihood of noise, wasted time, and disturbance to students still working. For that reason, many teachers use more efficient procedures such as having students place completed work on the corner of their desks or tables, or in conveniently-located baskets. The work is then collected by a teacher, aide, or student assistant.

The Use Of Student Assistants. It is strongly recommended that students in the class be assigned duties to help with routine procedures. Often called monitors or assistants, these students can do many of the time-consuming tasks typically done by teachers. In addition, responsibility for helping the classroom run smoothly often improves student attitudes toward the class.

At the secondary level, student assistants are most useful for distributing and collecting materials and for replenishing and taking care of supplies. They are frequently used, as well, for simple grading of papers, record keeping, typing, and duplicating materials. At the elementary level, teachers often assign tasks to every student in the class—for example, president, flag salute leader, lights monitor, window monitor, news and weather reporters, messenger, line monitors, group or table leaders, plant and pet caretakers, materials monitor, audiovisual assistants, visitor greeter, and so on. One can easily find enough jobs for all students. The jobs should be rotated so that all students participate at least occasionally.

Providing Assistance To Students At Work. As you recall from the Frederic Jones model, teachers are often quite inefficient in providing help to students doing seatwork. They tend to spend too much time with each student who raises a hand, while others students sit, often for several minutes, doing nothing or getting into trouble. Jones provided excellent advice on how to give help efficiently. As you probably remember, his suggestions included:

1. Make sure students know what they are supposed to do and how they are supposed to do it.
2. Leave a model on the board or a chart to which students can refer.
3. Circulate among students to check for progress and errors.
4. When students raise their hands, give them direct help and then move away quickly. Do this in twenty seconds or less. Do not let students become psychologically dependent on your presence before they will do their work. Reinforce those who work well on their own.
5. Do not succumb to the temptation to reteach individual students or take them through question and answer tutorials. If several students are having the same difficulty, consider stopping the activity and reteaching the concept or process to the entire class.

Communications Management

Teachers, already overburdened with the excessive work load of teaching, often give scant attention to communication. This is understandable, yet the fact is that communication, well-done and well-managed, returns a handsome yield on the time investment it requires, because it improves student attitude, reduces the amount of misbehavior, and increases support from parents.

Three different kinds of communication bring these desired results. The first is communication whose purpose is to *inform*. The second is communication whose purpose is to *solve problems* in the classroom. And the third has the purpose of *building positive student attitudes*. Let us see how each of the three is done.

Communication To Inform. Research has shown that teachers who take pains to present information about programs, expectations, and progress are held in higher esteem and receive more support than teachers who do not.

This type of communication is directed to students, parents, administrators, colleagues, and occasionally to the public. It deals with topics such as:

- The curriculum—the program and what it entails.
- Expectations of students and standards of conduct.

- Information concerning student progress.
- Casual information about forthcoming activities of interest.
- Special needs and help required for the class.

This type of informative communication is delivered by means of group presentations, written outlines, monthly class newsletters, notes and memos, telephone calls, and personal contacts. If you habituate yourself to providing this kind of communication routinely, you will find that it can be done with a minimum of time and effort. The payoff lies in better student attitude and behavior, increased parental appreciation and support, and increased support from administrators and colleagues.

Communication To Solve Problems. Earlier chapters presented many suggestions for solving classroom problems through effective communication. For example, one suggestion involved *clearly describing and discussing expectations concerning student conduct*, combined with the positive and negative consequences associated with good and bad behavior. Another had to do with *giving attention to the troublesome situation*, rather than attacking the student's character. Yet another had to do with holding *classroom meetings*, whose purpose was to explore problems and find solutions to them, without placing blame or verbally attacking others.

A problem-solving approach not described earlier is the *no-lose approach* popularized by Thomas Gordon, the widely acclaimed psychologist and author of *Teacher Effectiveness Training* (1974). This technique is used when the problem is one of personal conflict between two or more persons, and it allows all parties to emerge as "winners." Typically, says Gordon, conflict ultimately produces a winner and a loser, with the loser ending up hurt, frustrated, and vengeful. The no-lose approach calls on disputants to identify several possible solutions to their disagreement until they find one that seems to satisfy everyone concerned. They then try the solution to see if it works. If it does not, a new solution is identified and tried until everyone is able to accept the results.

Communication To Build Positive Attitudes. The main ways to help build positive student attitudes through communication are: (1) provide regular, positive personal attention, (2) show continual willingness to help, (3) focus on progress and the overcoming of obstacles, and (4) use what Eric Berne (1964) called "parallel communication," in which we use the adult ego-state when speaking with students.

The first three are self-explanatory; you have considered all of them before, at least briefly. Let it suffice here to say that if you are asked to identify the best teachers you ever had, it is likely that you will identify people who took a personal interest in you, held high standards for you, truly believed you could reach those standards, and with kindness helped you grow in ability, confidence, and self-esteem.

Concerning the fourth, parallel communication, it would be well to spend a moment reflecting on its meaning, implementation, and effects. Eric Berne, in his book *Games People Play* (1964), described three ego states that people typically reflect when interacting with others. He called those states the *parent*, *child*, and *adult* states, corresponding roughly to the familiar id, ego, and superego from Freudian psychodynamics. Berne described the three states as follows:

- *Parent*—talking to someone as our parents talked to us when we were children, that is, giving advice, correcting, admonishing, and controlling.
- *Child*—talking, acting, thinking, and feeling as we did when we were children, deferring to authority, behaving emotionally rather than rationally, and showing hurt feelings and pettiness.
- *Adult*—talking, acting, thinking, and reasoning in logical, rational ways. We do not moralize, preach, or admonish. Neither do we automatically defer to others. We communicate by considering the facts, sorting them out, organizing them, and expressing them firmly though not hostilely.

It is the adult state that is most effective in communication, especially if we want to build self-esteem in others. It is the state in which we show that we value the opinions and ideas of others. Thomas Harris, in his book *I'm O.K.—You're O.K.* (1967) put it this way: When you use the adult ego state in communicating with others, you convey the message that both you and the other person are O.K. But when you use either the parent or child state, you convey the message that one person is better than the other.

Conferencing with Parents

A fact of life is that all teachers must, sooner or later, conference with parents, either as a routine procedure or because they have had trouble with a particular student. Conferencing with parents is among the most anxiety-producing situations with which teachers must deal. They fear that criticism will be directed at their program, their judgment, their way of teaching, or in particular their way of dealing with a particular child. None of us likes such criticism; we detest having to defend ourselves or our work. The mere threat of it, even when it is unlikely to occur, is enough to cause fitful sleep and loss of appetite.

However, the purpose of such conferences is to improve the overall educational progress of the child. If you can keep that essential point in mind, and if you prepare adequately for the conference, you will find that nine times out of ten the meeting will be both pleasant and productive.

Preparing For The Parent Conference. By preparing adequately in advance, you greatly increase the likelihood that you will make a positive impression and that the conference will be pleasant and productive. Keep these things in mind as you prepare:

1. Have the student's strengths and weaknesses clearly in mind.
2. Prepare a folder for the student, with the student's name written on it attractively.
3. Include a summary of your program, showing work completed and work yet to be done.
4. Include samples of the student's work.
5. Have available grades and tests that back up your evaluation.
6. Anticipate questions parents are most likely to ask:
   How does my child get along with others?
   Does my child cause problems?
   Is my child progressing as well as expected?
   What are my child's specific needs?
   Is there anything you want me to do to help?

Conducting The Conference. Secure in the preparation you have made in advance, you can free your mind to concentrate on conducting the conference professionally, with taste and tact. The following add to the professional tone of the conference:

1. Think of yourself in the parent's place. Be tactful and polite.
2. Greet the parent in a friendly, relaxed manner.
3. Sit side by side with the parent at a table, rather than on opposite sides of a desk.
4. Begin by chatting about the student as a worthwhile person. Mention good traits. This reassures the parent.
5. Guide the parent through the student's file, commenting on samples of work included. Refer to tests and grades if appropriate.
6. Encourage the parent to talk. Listen carefully and be accepting. Do not argue or criticize; this causes resentment. Parents cannot be objective about their child.
7. Let the parent know that you both want the best education for the child.
8. End the conference by describing your plans for the student's future progress. Earnestly request the parent's support. Thank the parent for meeting with you to talk about the child.

Reminder: Elements in Good Communication

In this chapter and elsewhere, certain elements of effective communication have been described. The following list serves as a reminder for the most effective communication:

- *Clarity*—Say what you mean to say, in an organized, logical way, using understandable language.
- *Professional Demeanor*—Be friendly yet businesslike; do not gossip or talk for talk's sake.
- *Positive Approach*—Use messages that produce positive feelings and build self-concept.
- *Assertiveness*—Make sure you express your points in a friendly, insistent way, not giving in to others when you need to stick to your ground.
- *Flexibility*—Be ready to change your mind or admit mistakes when necessary.
- *The Two-Way Test*—Evaluate what you are going to say in terms of the two-way test: Is it true? Will it help? If it doesn't pass both parts of the test, don't say it.

Application Exercises

1. Examine this contribution from teacher Colleen Meagher and identify management that has to do with physical environment, psychosocial environment, and routines.

   I arrange things so that the daily schedule flows more smoothly and I don't have to give unnecessary directions. Transitions are timed with a kitchen timer and the class is challenged to see if they can quietly clean up and prepare for the next activity before it rings. I allow the students to work in cooperative groups and at times allow them to talk quietly and move about the room. Traffic patterns are clearly defined. Desks are arranged in a U-shape facing the chalkboard, so I have eye contact and easy access to all students.

2. Mr. Tales, a colleague of yours, has prepared the following note to send to parents describing his goals for the class:

   We will be working to maximize self-image through both traditional and newer effective approaches. Intended learnings will be stated in terms of experiences rather than behaviorally. Assessment of progress will be accomplished observationally. Your input into this process will be valued.

   Mr. Tales asks you to look over the note and make suggestions before he sends it out. What do you suggest to him?

3. For a grade, subject, and topic you select, describe how you would

manage materials distribution and collection, work routines, and assistance for students during independent or group work.

4. For a grade or subject you select, describe what you would want to
   communicate to parents and how you would communicate with them.
   Be realistic in terms of time required.

5. You are preparing for a conference with the father of James, a de-
   lightfully humorous and well-intentioned boy who is barely passing
   his course work. His study habits are poor in school and, you suspect,
   nonexistent at home. The principal has informed you that James's
   father requires that James work in their upholstery shop after school
   hours. What will you say to the father, and how will you proceed?

6. You are preparing to conference with the mother of Alouette, a pain-
   fully shy girl who gets teased by other students because of the old-
   fashioned clothes she wears. You know that the family has little
   money. You want to tell the mother that Alouette's clothes are
   causing problems in the class. You remember to apply the two-way
   test before speaking. What do you then decide to say or do?

REFERENCES

Berne, E. (1964). *Games people play*. New York: Grove.

Brophy, J. (1985). Classroom management as instruction: socializing self-guidance
in students. *Theory Into Practice, 24*, 233–240.

Charles, C. (1983). *Elementary classroom management*. New York: Longman.

Emmer, E., Evertson, C., Clements, B., & Worsham, M. (1984). *Classroom
management for secondary teachers*. Englewood Cliffs, NJ: Prentice-Hall.

Evertson, C., Emmer, E., Clements, B., Sanford, J., Worsham, M., & Williams,
E. (1981). *Organizing and managing the elementary school classroom*. Report
No. 6060. Austin: University of Texas, Research and Development Center for
Teacher Education.

Evertson, C., & Emmer, E. (1982). Effective management at the beginning of
the school year in junior high classes. *Journal of Educational Psychology, 74*,
485–498.

Evertson, C. (1986). Training teachers in classroom management: an experimental
study in secondary school classrooms. *Journal of Educational Research, 79*,
51–58.

Fifer, F. (1986). Effective classroom management. *Academic Therapy, 21*,
401–410.

Gordon, T. (1974). *Teacher effectiveness training*. New York: McKay.

CHAPTER 11

Building a Personal
System of Discipline

The ultimate purpose of this book is to help you build and implement an effective system of discipline—one that takes into account the ages and personalities of the students you teach as well as your own philosophy and personal preferences. Teachers have always developed personal systems of discipline, but until recently they lacked systematic guidance from researcher-specialists in school discipline. All too often teachers had no sure way of enforcing their requirements. Students took advantage when teachers tried to be friendly and gentle. In order to be successful, teachers resorted to stern treatment, backed with the threat of punishment.

That uneasy standoff still depicts many classrooms, where students and teachers act as adversaries, each a bit fearful and distrusting of the other. But as the preceding chapters have shown, teachers no longer have to waste psychic energy and precious instructional time attempting to deal with inconsiderate students bent on devilry. They have at their disposal proven methods of guiding student behavior in positive directions. This information is available for the taking; teachers need no longer fear that their personal and professional lives will be ruined by misbehaving students.

But of course that helpful information must be put into practice. The major question for teachers today is not whether they can have discipline but, rather, how they can combine what is known about discipline into effective systems that meet both their needs and those of their students (Ban, 1986). You might think that the simplest thing would be to examine existing models of discipline and select the best. The solution, however, is not so easy. For example, behavior modification may work wonderfully well with young and some handicapped students, but not so well with older students and those inclined to rowdiness. Assertive discipline, while effective in controlling misbehavior at all levels, may seem too cumbersome for primary grades and may not satisfy teachers concerned with helping students begin to value proper behavior. And so it is with the other models, all of which have special strengths, but also limitations.

Thus, despite having at hand so much information and proven technique, teachers still have the necessity (or might one say the opportunity?) to build their own personal systems of discipline that they believe best for themselves and the students they teach. They can do this by selecting from among the various models those elements that suit them best and recombining them into an effective approach that is satisfactory to all (Purvis & Leonard, 1985.).

PART 1. BACKGROUND FOR BUILDING YOUR SYSTEM OF DISCIPLINE

What Teachers Want

Most teachers want a system of discipline that effectively provides the following:

1. Prevention of student misbehavior.
2. Positive control of misbehavior when it does occur.
3. Student growth toward valuing better behavior.
4. Growth in positive, trusting relationships between teacher and students.
5. Parental support and assistance in building self-discipline.

Review this list to see if it describes what you want from your system of discipline. Modify the list as needed so you can use it as a guide in building your own personal system.

What Teachers Can Expect from Students

Students as a group behave in fairly predictable ways. Their patterns of group behavior have been described by numerous psychologists and sociologists, and most experienced teachers have learned those patterns first hand. Individual behavior within the groups is not so predictable, yet enough is known to allow us to make generalizations useful in building personal systems of discipline. Here are some of the things you can expect from your students:

1. *Students are going to misbehave in school.* Most beginning teachers hope fervently they will encounter no misbehavior; some even believe they will not. But misbehavior is a fact of classroom life. The discipline system you build should reduce misbehavior considerably and should give you the ability to deal with it positively without trauma to you or your students.

2. *Students need discipline.* Students, like all the rest of us, would often rather goof-off than work, rather talk than keep quiet, rather interact humorously (or naughtily) with others than work individually. Yet much school work requires attention, diligence, quiet, and individual effort. And a major goal of schooling is to help students develop self-discipline and approved social behavior. Your discipline system will help students do those things necessary to furthering their education while limiting those behaviors that are self-defeating.

3. *All students seek acceptance, belonging, success, and enjoyment.* Most social behavior in the classroom can be linked to the students' attempts to gain acceptance, feel a sense of belonging, and see themselves as successful. They do not always know how to attain those ends, and they often misbehave as a result. They often misbehave even when they do know what is acceptable and not. Your discipline system should be organized to assist students in reaching these primary goals in acceptable ways.

4. *All students can behave acceptably; it is a matter of choice, and students make their own decisions.* Given a good classroom climate for learning, there is no excuse for student misbehavior. Students behave the way they do either because they don't know better or because their misbehavior is being reinforced by other students (or sometimes just because they don't care much about themselves or anything else in life). Your system of discipline should give students every opportunity and encouragement to behave well, and it should give positive redirection to misbehavior that does occur.

Solace for Teachers

Teachers see discipline as an onerous task and fervently wish they never had to deal with it. This is certainly understandable, but wishing doesn't make the problem go away. You can ease the burden by taking cognizance of the following truths, which should be kept in mind as you build your system of discipline:

1. *Students require discipline.* They must have it for positive social development and for adequate educational progress. That point has already been made.
2. *The teacher is the most important figure in establishing class discipline.* You will be wise to involve students and their parents in the process of putting your system of discipline into practice. But it is you who sets the tone, establishes the expectations, enforces the rules, and continually strives to help students avoid self-destructive behavior. You may not enjoy doing this, but remember that it is one of the most important things you can do for your students. They will respect and even appreciate you for doing so.
3. *One of the best ways to teach good behavior is through example.* One of the nicest things about teaching is the opportunity to associate with quality people. That allows you to behave in keeping with your own personal standards of quality and thereby influence your students as well. Your students will imitate you to a surprising extent. If you are kind and respectful, students will tend to follow your lead, but if you are negative and sarcastic, they will follow that lead as well.
4. *Teachers cannot teach well without discipline.* More than anything else, teachers want to be able to teach students the school curriculum, with students attentive, cooperative, and appreciative. Your system of discipline is the key to your being able to teach in this way. You know by now that most classrooms without effective discipline become chaotic or as mean as prisons. Therefore, if you want to teach well you must maintain effective discipline.

The Importance of Rights in the Classroom

Thanks to Lee Canter's admonitions, educators are coming to speak of "basic rights" in the classroom. These rights are not civil, legal, or "human." They should be thought of as "educational rights." They describe conditions that all classroom participants are entitled to expect. Students, administrators, and parents all have parts to play in securing these rights, but it is the primary responsibility of the teacher to see to it that they are put into operation. Keep these rights continually in mind, for they furnish much of the infrastructure upon which you build your personal system of discipline.

Students' Rights. Students are considered to have three educational rights in the classroom, rights to which they are entitled and which they should expect, but which unfortunately they do not always enjoy. Those three rights are:

1. The right to a learning environment that is appropriately well-ordered, peaceful, safe, nonthreatening, and conducive to learning.
2. The right to have a caring, well-prepared teacher who instructs well and who limits students' inappropriate self-destructive behavior.
3. The right to choose how to behave, with full understanding of the consequences that invariably follow the choices.

Teachers' Rights. Keep in mind too, as you prepare your system of discipline, that you are entitled to certain rights in the classroom. You should insist, for the good of everyone concerned, that your rights are maintained. Your classroom rights include:

1. The right to establish optimal learning environments that are consonant with your individual strengths and limitations.
2. The right to teach in ways that meet the learning and behavioral needs of the students in your classes.
3. The right to expect behavior from students that contributes to their optimal growth, while also meeting your needs.
4. The right to teach in a climate that is free from disruptions.
5. The right to ask and receive help and backing from administrators and parents.

Without these rights of students and teachers, quality instruction cannot be maintained over the long haul. But with them, teachers are freed to instruct in accord with their talents while students are freed to concentrate on learning in accord with their potentials.

PART 2. BUILDING YOUR SYSTEM OF DISCIPLINE

Three Faces of Discipline

To begin building your system of discipline, it is helpful to think of discipline as having three facets—three faces. Those three faces are: (1) *preventive discipline*, (2) *supportive discipline*, and (3) *corrective discipline*. The labels suggest the different aspects of classroom discipline, each of which is very important in a well-rounded system of discipline. You will want to give attention to each facet. The following sections describe the facets and present selected strategies you may want to consider incorporating into them.

Preventive Discipline. Preventive discipline has to do with forestalling misbehavior, with preventing it from occurring in the first place. Teachers have found that preventing misbehavior is much better for all concerned than having to deal with it after it has occurred—the old ounce of prevention being worth a pound of cure. You hear it said that the best way to prevent misbehavior is to make sure you provide a very interesting curriculum, where students become so involved in learning that it never occurs to them to misbehave. If there is a chance that might fall short, teachers have been advised to get their bluff in from the start so students won't dare to cross them.

Actually, there is truth in both these adages, especially that concerning good, interesting curriculum. Interesting curriculum certainly cuts down on the incidence of misbehavior. And for a time at least, a tough hostile attitude on the part of the teacher can work—but only for a time; the bad effects on student attitude and self-discipline soon outweigh the benefits.

Fortunately, there are a number of specific things you can do to reduce the likelihood of misbehavior. Each of those presented here has the additional advantage of building positive relationships and fostering a more positive attitude toward school.

The following preventive strategies should be considered as you build your system of discipline:

1. *Make your curriculum as worthwhile and enjoyable as possible.* Select worthwhile learnings and provide enjoyable activities. Keep in mind students' basic needs for fun, belonging, freedom, and power.
2. *Take charge in your classroom.* Every authority on discipline agrees that teachers must take charge firmly in their classes. They should be pleasant, but at the same time forceful. They ask for student input, but they make the final decisions.
3. *Make good rules for class conduct.* Rules should be short and clear. Five or six are enough. Discuss them carefully with students, then post them in the room and review them from time to time.
4. *Stress good manners and living by the golden rule.* Make it plain from the outset that you care enough about your students to expect the highest standards of behavior from them. Expect them to use good manners. Prohibit sarcasm and cruelty. Be the best model you can, by showing concern, manners, courtesy, and helpfulness. Discuss this point frequently and call attention to improvements.

Supportive Discipline. Misbehavior seldom starts with bad intentions. All students at times become restive, squabble, have difficulties, encounter disappointments, fall under the charismatic spell of misbehaving peers, cannot resist the impulse to talk and laugh, or for myriad untold reasons simply feel like kicking up their heels.

It is when these kinds of behaviors first appear that supportive discipline is brought into play. As the label indicates, this type of discipline simply helps students maintain self-control. It employs subtle techniques for helping students get back to work. Often, only the student toward whom the techniques are directed knows they have been used. The following strategies are suggested for supportive discipline:

1. *Use signals directed to a student needing support.* Learn to catch students' eyes and use head shakes, frowns, and hand signals to direct them back to work.
2. *Use physical proximity when signals are ineffective.* This is simply moving near the student, which is usually more than enough to revive interest in the work at hand.
3. *Show interest in student work.* Move alongside students who show signs of restlessness, look at their work, ask cheerful questions or make favorable comments about it, and sometimes give a light challenge: "You have done a great deal of this already. I bet you can't get five more done before we stop."
4. *Restructure difficult work or help with it.* Quickly spot students who seem to be having difficulties. Give a hint, clue, or direct suggestion that solves their problem. You may need at times to restructure an activity—change it in midstream, add excitement, or reduce the level of difficulty.
5. *Interject humor into lessons that have become tiring.* Students place high value on humor in their teachers. Humor provides a lift, a respite from tension. A momentary break is all that is needed. You must be careful, though, that the humor does not provoke joking and horseplay that can effectively put an end to a lesson before the work is completed.
6. *Remove seductive objects.* A great variety of nonschool objects regularly appears in the classroom—toys, comics, rubber bands, animals, notes, and numerous unmentionables. They intrigue students and draw them away from the lesson. Ask students to put such objects away. If they do not, take possession of them yourself without fuss, then return them to the owners (accompanied by a few pointed comments) at the end of the period or day.
7. *Reinforce good behavior, in appropriate ways at appropriate times.* This should be done informally, with nods, smiles, and words such as "Thanks," "Good," "Keep it up." Compliment students when they show good effort, but be careful not to single out individual students for praise in front of their peers. Reinforce as a group as much as possible.
8. *Request good behavior.* Use suggestions, hints, and I-messages as students begin to drift toward misbehavior. Show that you recognize

the trying situation: "You have worked so hard, and we are all getting tired. Please give me five more minutes of your best attention and we will be able to finish."

Corrective Discipline. You will find that despite your best efforts at preventive and supportive discipline, some misbehavior will still occur. When students violate rules, when they choose self-defeating behavior, it is your unpleasant duty to stop and redirect their misbehavior. This corrective discipline is what most people envision when they think of classroom discipline—students act awful and the teacher reacts with scowls, blazing tongue, and willow rod.

Enlightened corrective discipline bears little resemblance to that stereotype. Good corrective discipline is neither harshly intimidating nor punitive. It is relatively nontraumatic, intended to stop the misbehavior and redirect it positively. Consider the following strategies for the corrective facet of your personal system of discipline:

1. *Assertively insist on these rights in the classroom—your right to teach without disruptions and the students' right to learn.* Explain what these ideas mean and give hypothetical examples of violations. When students begin to misbehave, reassert the rights.
2. *Stop the misbehavior.* It is best to put an immediate end to the misbehavior rather than ignore it and hope it will go away. If the behavior is a gross violation of rules or decorum—fighting or loud swearing, for example—it must be squelched immediately: "Johnny, there is no swearing in this class!" Or "Boys, come with me at once to the office!" Milder misbehavior can be stopped by putting names and checks on the board as Canter suggests or by a number of other techniques described in the various models.
3. *Invoke the consequences tied to the misbehavior.* If you have explained your rules and the consequences for breaking them, your students come to understand that they are choosing how to behave and that they are also choosing the consequences that automatically accompany their behavior. No need to get upset; just say, "Susan, you have chosen not to complete your work, so you must stay after school until you complete it."
4. *Follow through consistently.* Make sure you invoke consequences the same way day after day. Being stern one day and lax the next only leaves students confused and encourages them to test your rules. Don't let students talk you out of the consequences they have chosen; if you do, it encourages them to test you again.
5. *Redirect misbehavior in positive directions.* This is a strategy on which all authorities agree. Ask students who have misbehaved to

state what they should do instead. Provide choices if they have difficulty expressing themselves. A major purpose of classroom discipline is to teach students how to behave better and encourage them to do so.

Toward Balanced Discipline Your Way

The ideas you have considered in this book should have convinced you that classroom discipline is necessary to successful teaching and learning, that you can develop an effective yet humane system of classroom discipline, and that you can structure your system to meet your students' needs as well as your own. The three faces of preventive, supportive, and corrective discipline, when combined, give you a balanced system, one with which you and your students can live happily. All that remains is to tailor your system to your specifications. You should be able to accomplish this final task through the following steps:

To Plan and Initiate Your System

1. *Specify your needs and set your limits.* While keeping in mind your students' needs, carefully consider your own needs as well. Then specify the behavior limits that permit both sets of needs to be met. In taking this step, most teachers consider such matters as talk, movement, noise, self-control, beginning and completing work, and personal manners.

2. *Write out rules that state the limits.* State your rules positively, when possible. Limit their number to five or six and put them on a chart that can be displayed in your classroom.

3. *Determine the consequences that accompany your rules, when followed and when broken.* Focus on having students do correctly whatever they have done incorrectly.

4. *Decide specifically what you will do with regard to preventive, supportive, and corrective aspects of discipline.* Emphasize preventive and supportive discipline; they make school much more enjoyable and profitable for you and your students. But be sure you build reliable corrective measures into your system; they are indispensable.

5. *Establish your support system.* Take your plan to the principal, explain it, and ask for support. If the principal cannot support it, decide mutually what can be changed, because you must have the principal's support. Discuss the plan with a fellow teacher and arrange mutual support.

6. *Give thought to how you can build a positive classroom climate that will help students with their own self-control.*

7. *Discuss rules and consequences with students the very first day.* Make sure everyone understands your system. Emphasize classroom rights to teach and learn. Stress that students have choices, and that consequences invariably accompany those choices.

To Test Your System
1. *Put the system into effect as planned.*
2. During the first week *assess your system* in terms of: (a) its effectiveness in controlling misbehavior, (b) its ease of implementation, and (c) its contribution to a positive classroom climate.
3. For fourth grade and higher, *discuss your assessment* with the students. Consider any input they may give but reserve the right to make final decisions about changes.
4. *Modify your system if necessary.* Explain to the students why you are making the changes.

To Maintain and Strengthen Your System
1. *Work to enliven and smooth out your curriculum.* Provide work that is worthwhile and interesting. Establish classroom procedures that produce smooth flow, with few dead spots and little confusion.
2. *Be the best possible model for your students.* Act as you want them to act; speak as you want them to speak.
3. *Interact with students on a personal level.* Talk with them. Show interest in them. Help with their difficulties.
4. *Help students choose good behavior.* Have them make judgments about their behavior. Suggest alternatives. Reinforce good behavior. Make sure good behavior brings better consequences than does bad behavior.
5. *Never give up.* Even when the going gets tough; even when you are demoralized; even when students don't seem to appreciate your efforts. Rest secure in the knowledge that through your discipline system you are giving your students the best help they are likely to get.

A Model System

How might a system look when prepared according to these guidelines? Wide variations are possible, of course, because of the differences in needs, philosophies, and situations among teachers. One possibility is shown in the following model, prepared by Deborah Sund for use at the elementary level and presented here with her permission. (Six additional discipline plans of actual teachers at other levels and subjects are presented in Chapter 12.)

THE SUND MODEL

My Needs, Likes, and Dislikes

My Needs

1. Orderly classroom appearance—good room arrangement, materials neatly stored, interesting, well-thought-out displays.
2. Structure and routines—set schedule, with flexibility, allowing for teacher improvisation when needed.
3. Transitions—smooth between activities, with no wasted time.
4. Attention—student attention for directions and given to all speakers and instructional activities.
5. Situational—appropriate behaviors—quietly attentive during instruction, considerate interaction during group activities, and so forth.

My Likes

1. Enthusiasm—from me and my students.
2. Warmth—as reflected in mutual regard among all individuals in the class.
3. Positive, relaxed classroom environment—reflecting self-control, mutual helpfulness, assumption of responsibility.

My Dislikes

1. Inattention to speaker, teacher, other adult, or class member.
2. Excessive noise—loud voices, inappropriate talking, and laughing.
3. Distractions in the form of toys, unnecessary movement, poking, teasing, etc.
4. Misusing, wasting, or destroying instructional materials.
5. Unkind behavior—verbal or physical abuse of others in the classroom.
6. Rude conduct—ridicule, sarcasm, bad manners.
7. Tattling.

My Classroom Rules

The following are my classroom rules, together with indications of how I would explain them to my students.

1. Be considerate of others at all times. (Speak kindly, be helpful, don't bother others.)
2. Do your best work. (Get as much done as you can. Do your work neatly, so you can be proud of it. Don't waste time.)
3. Use quiet voices in the classroom. (Use regular speaking voices during class discussions. Speak quietly during cooperative work groups. Whisper at other times if you need help.)
4. Use signals to request permission or receive help. (Explain the signal systems for assistance, movement, restroom pass.)

The rules are discussed and agreed to by the students on the first day of school. After the students have familiarized themselves with the rules and routines, I continue to give them prompts, cues, hints, and other assistance in practicing adherence to the rules.

Positive Consequences

As students follow the rules, they know they will routinely receive the following positive consequences:

1. Positive verbal feedback.
2. Positive nonverbal feedback (smiles, winks, nods, pats).
3. Occasional tangible and privilege awards (stickers, marks, favorite activities).
4. Positive reports to parents (notes, phone calls).

Negative Consequences

When students do not abide by the rules, they know they will routinely receive the following negative consequences:

1. "Pirate eyes"—a stern glance, accompanied by a disappointed and puzzled expression.
2. Unapproving general comments—"I hear noise." "Some people are not listening."
3. Direct negative verbal feedback—"Gordon, you did not use the signal. Please use the signal."
4. A Canter system of names and checks on the board.
5. Unfavorable reports to parents (note, call, school conference).
6. In-class isolation—student separated from group but still in sight of teacher.
7. Student sent to principal or counselor or removed from the class.

My Preventive Discipline Measures

I take the following steps to minimize the occurrence of behavior problems in my classroom:

1. Involve students in establishing class rules and assuming responsibility. In discussions I ask questions such as:
   "What do you think happens when everyone tries to talk at the same time?"
   "How do you like other people to speak to you?"
2. Make contact with parents. I do the following:
   Send letters outlining expectations and discipline system.
   Make short, positive phone calls to parents.
   Send notes with children concerning good work and behavior.
3. Organize a classroom environment for best temperature, light, and comfort, with traffic patterns for efficient movement within the room.

4. Stress, model, and hold practice sessions on good manners, courtesy, and responsibility.
5. Provide a varied, active curriculum with opportunities for physical movement, singing, interaction, and so forth.
6. Provide a sense of consistency, familiarity, and security, through structure and routines.

My Supportive Discipline Measures

In order to help my students support their own self-control when I see them beginning to drift, I use the following supportive measures:

1. Eye contact; facial expressions.
2. Physical proximity.
3. Refer to classroom rules.
4. Show interest in individual students' work.
5. Modify the lesson or routine if needed to increase interest or reduce anxiety.
6. Use behavior modification—rewards for perseverence.

My Corrective Discipline Measures

When, despite my best preventive and supportive efforts, students misbehave anyway, I use the following corrective measures:

1. Comment on misbehavior. "I hear talking. I don't like it. Everyone should be listening."
2. Emphatic verbot. "Stop that now!"
3. Canter system of names and checks on board, linked to consequences of which the students are well aware.
4. Isolation of the student from the group.
5. Removal of the student to the principal or counselor's office.
6. Parental contacts by telephone.

My Way of Maintaining a Positive Classroom Climate

I have found that a positive climate results in better feelings, more enjoyment, and ultimately better self-control for both the students and myself. The following are some of the things I do to maintai. such a climate:

1. Respecting each child as an individual who is entitled to a good education.
2. Looking for the good or likable qualities in each child.
3. Acknowledging appropriate behavior, good work, effort, and improvement.
4. Taking time to get to know students better.
5. Giving out as many nonverbal positive responses as possible—winks, nods, smiles.
6. Taking time each day to assess student feelings.

7. Talking with students in ways that imply their own competence—
   e.g., "OK, you know what to do next."
8. Providing interesting and fun activities that are challenging, but
   at which students can succeed.
9. End each day on a positive note, with a fond goodbye and hope
   for a happy and productive tomorrow.

And What of Schoolwide Systems of Discipline?

Today a great many schools across the country have established schoolwide
discipline programs, where all teachers in the school use the same system
of discipline (Pinnell, et al., 1982). This movement, intended to make
discipline more consistent and effective, began to gain momentum in
the middle 1980s, fueled by the nationwide push for "effective schools,"
characterized as providing:

- A safe and orderly environment for learning.
- High standards and expectations.
- Opportunities for student involvement and responsibility.
- Emphasis on positive behavior and preventive discipline.

If you should teach in such a school, you would be expected to follow
the schoolwide discipline plan. You would be certain, however, to find
yourself using techniques advocated in the models presented in this book.
While it would be impossible to present here the varieties of discipline
systems that schools have developed, it is possible to categorize them into
three general types—single power systems (secondary), single power
systems (elementary), and combination systems (elementary).

Single Power Systems: Secondary Level. A power system is one that contains procedures for firmly stopping misbehavior and consistently invoking
consequences. Assertive discipline is an example of a power system. Power
systems may be distinguished from "softer" systems, such as behavior
modification, that provide influence through more subtle means such as
modeling and persuasion.

Most schoolwide systems at the secondary level are single power
systems, that is, one strong system is used by all teachers and other personnel in the school. The system has three main components: (1) a policy
concerning discipline that is established by the school board and then dis-
seminated to the school and community, (2) rules for student conduct, and
(3) enforcement procedures, consequences, and follow through.

Component one, the *school board policy*, describes: (1) the district's
philosophy concerning the relationship of discipline to education, (2) the

student responsibilities at school and in the educational program, (3) the teachers' responsibilities for communicating clear standards and consequences and consistently implementing them, (4) the administrators' responsibilities in communicating and enforcing discipline, (5) a list of prohibited behaviors, such as use of drugs and alcohol, destruction of property, fighting, and so forth, and (6) the consequences that will be invoked for violations of the rules.

Component two in the power system is *rules of student conduct*. Rules have been discussed repeatedly in previous chapters. For secondary schools, schoolwide rules are usually similar to the following list:

1. Always be on time and ready to work.
2. Treat all people and property with respect.
3. Cooperate with those in positions of authority.
4. Leave nuisance objects at home.
5. Do not disrupt the teaching-learning process.

Frequently, all school personnel, including librarians, secretaries, bus drivers, cafeteria workers, custodians, and so forth are empowered to enforce the rules.

Component three, *enforcement, consequences, and follow through*, involves the following measures.

1. All students are carefully made aware of the rules, consequences, and enforcement procedures. Charts displaying the rules are posted in classrooms and elsewhere in the school.
2. When a student violates a rule, a verbal warning is given. This warning carries no penalty. If the student misbehaves again, the person in authority makes a notation on a special form in triplicate —one copy goes to the student, a second to the office, and the third is kept by the person writing the complaint.
3. School counselors keep a conduct card for all students assigned to them. When the counselor receives a note indicating misbehavior, that infraction is entered on the student's conduct card.
4. Consequences are imposed on the student, beginning with restitutions and progressing on to detention, conferences with the teacher, referral to the counselor, calling the parent, referral to the vice principal, and loss of normal privileges such as attendance at dances, taking a class trip, or participation in athletic events. Always in effect is a "severe clause," which allows immediate referral to the principal and suspension from school for such acts as fighting and using drugs.

Single Power Systems: Elementary Level. Single power systems are occasionally used at the elementary level. A widely-used example is Canter's Assertive Discipline, which is very effective in suppressing misbehavior even at the kindergarten level. Most primary teachers do not approve of single power systems, however, considering them too harsh and too focused on punishing misbehavior rather than teaching proper behavior. Teachers who believe in assertive discipline counter that argument by insisting that such programs give students a feeling of consistency. They add that nothing prevents teachers from teaching good behavior along with the system.

Combination Systems: Elementary Level. Often favored in elementary schools are combinations of power systems and persuasive systems. Typically, persuasive and redirective techniques are used with primary grade children who are still in the process of learning what are and are not acceptable behaviors. This learning occurs best through good example combined with reinforcement and reteaching.

By the end of the primary grades students have become fully aware of the difference between acceptable and unacceptable behavior. At the same time, they fall progressively more under the influence of peers. Therefore, many schools use a stronger system of discipline for students in fourth grade and higher.

Rules at the elementary level tend to be rather more specific than those listed for the secondary level. They usually name specific behaviors such as staying in one's seat, raising hands before speaking, and so forth.

The power aspect of the combination system differs somewhat from that described as typical for high schools. At these earlier grades, strong emphasis remains on positive reinforcement for good behavior. Parents are often asked to assist at home in reinforcing good behavior and work and study habits. Enforcement procedures for misbehavior are carried out mainly by the classroom teacher. Counselors are seldom used.

Disagreements About Schoolwide Systems. As with all human endeavors that involve more than one person, disagreement occurs concerning schoolwide systems. While most teachers acknowledge the benefits of schoolwide systems, many claim that overall student behavior is no better than when teachers take care of the problems on their own. This is especially true for teachers who have been successful with discipline. They resent giving up their effective approaches to turn to a system about which they are unsure.

Teachers complain too of weariness of years of administrative press for solutions to school problems, only to see after much work and effort that conditions are no better than before. This feeling must be addressed when schools attempt to put new discipline systems into place. The best way to address the problem is to allow teachers to visit other schools where such systems are used effectively and talk with teachers and students about their reactions.

Finally, there is the old "still more extra work" bugaboo that has become an almost insupportable burden for teachers. Teachers already suffer from very high levels of stress, much of which is brought about by too much to do and too little time in which to get it done. They automatically equate new plans with more work, taking a stance of rejection until proven wrong. Yet it is evident that teachers will willingly work on new systems that bring benefits to both their students and to themselves. Once persuaded that schoolwide systems of discipline are more effective while requiring no more work from teachers, they tend to endorse them wholeheartedly.

Comment on Schoolwide Systems

Schoolwide systems of discipline do not improve class control of stronger teachers, but they do seem to improve student behavior in classrooms of teachers who have difficulty with control, as well as in other areas of the school such as library, shops, cafeteria, grounds, buses, and so forth. Moreover, the community tends to stand strongly behind schoolwide systems, appreciating both the school's attempt to provide positive learning climates and the consistency the program brings. If you would like more information on schoolwide systems, you can obtain a listing of schools recognized across the country for outstanding discipline programs. This list is available from Phi Delta Kappa (PDK Commission on Discipline, Eighth and Union, Box 789, Bloomington, Indiana 47402).

Application Exercises

1. Specify what you as a teacher consider acceptable with regard to noise, talk, movement, and courtesy. Formulate your statements into class rules.
2. To what extent does your own experience confirm or deny the following statements:
   All students need discipline.
   All students can choose to behave acceptably.
   Teachers cannot teach well if they cannot maintain discipline.
   Teachers have a right to teach, free from disruptions.
   Students have a right to learn, free from disruptions.
3. What relative weightings would you place on preventive, supportive, and corrective discipline in your personal system?
4. Outline your personal system of discipline to include at least the following:
   Your needs, likes, and dislikes

Rules
Consequences, positive and negative
Preventive measures
Supportive measures
Corrective measures
Support team
Your way of maintaining a positive classroom climate
Your way of helping students build their own self-control.

REFERENCES

Ban, J. (1986). School discipline: in pursuit of a system. *High School Journal 69*, 6–11. October/November.
Pinnell, G., Lasley, T., Wayson, W., & Wynn, G. (1982). *Directory of schools reported to have exemplary discipline*. Bloomington, IN: Phi Delta Kappa.
Purvis, J., & Leonard, R. (1985). Content for a student discipline course. *Education*, *106*, 94–101.

CHAPTER 12

Exemplars: Personal Systems of Discipline

Chapter 11 presented guidelines to help you build your own personal system of discipline. To provide you with further insights and assistance, this chapter presents samples of personal discipline systems that were developed using those same guidelines. These systems were all composed and used by real teachers who have been kind enough to allow their work to be included here. Presented are two systems used at high school level, two at intermediate grade level, two at primary grade level, and two "specialty systems."

TWO HIGH SCHOOL SYSTEMS

High School System #1:

Teacher: Leslie Hays
Subject: Physical Science

My personal belief is that every one of my students can behave appropriately in my classroom every day. My personal goal is to be an effective teacher for them. I try to accomplish this through clarity, firmness, and a human touch. It is very important to me to establish a sense of class belonging and unity, with shared objectives and goals. Toward that end I try to inject humor and fun, and I find that student participation follows naturally.

At the same time I concentrate on preventive and supportive discipline by doing extensive planning and by constantly monitoring each of my students. This frees me from having to deal continually with misbehavior. I communicate with parents by note and telephone, and most of them are so thankful that I have called them to talk about their child, they become my allies in class control.

My students range from remedial (almost always considered behavior problems) to advanced. With all levels, my discipline plan works best for me with a very structured approach that communicates my standards and requirements.

My plan goes into effect within the first five minutes of class each September. Each individual is given a class behavior contract, which must be taken home, signed by their parents, and returned to me the next day. If they bring it back when due, I give them points. If they are a day late, they get no points, and if it doesn't come back the third day I call the parents at home. The contract outlines my philosophy and behavior guidelines:

Dear Student and Parent:

In order to guarantee all the students in my classroom the excellent learning climate they deserve, I am utilizing the following discipline plan.

Attendance: Attendance is essential to the learning process. You cannot expect to succeed if you do not participate in the daily activity of the classroom. Therefore, after a student's fourth absence, the parent will be notified. After 15 absences, the student will be subject to failure in the class.

Tardies: Students are expected to be in their assigned seat and ready to begin work when the final bell rings. A student/parent warning is issued after two tardies. After four tardies a letter will be sent home. Following the seventh tardy, you are subject to being dropped from the class with an F. Citizenship grades will be lowered one grade for every two tardies.

Class Behavior: I believe that all my students can behave appropriately in my classroom. I will not tolerate a student stopping me from teaching or preventing any other student from learning.

Class Rules:
1. Bring your science book, notebook, and pencil every day. I DON'T LEND ANYTHING.
2. Be attentive while the teacher, or a student who is called on, is talking.
3. Bring no food, drink, candy, gum, hats, or sunglasses to the class.
4. Handle all equipment properly.
5. Profanity and verbal abuse are not tolerated.
6. Remain in your seat at the end of the period until dismissed by the teacher.

Consequences: High citizenship and conduct grades will be awarded to those students who contribute positively to the daily activities of the classroom.

If on the other hand a student chooses to interfere with learning process, the following consequences will be invoked:

- First time: Warning—mark on discipline card.
- Second time: Notify parent of behavior problem.
- Third time: Referral to counselor.
- Fourth time: Referral to vice principal for disciplinary action.
- Students who write on desks or throw trash around the room will be assigned immediate after-school detention to clean *all* of the desk tops and *all* of the trash.
- *Note: More serious problems such as defiance, fighting, theft, abuse of equipment, or violation of laboratory safety rules will result in immediate referral to the vice principal.

It is in the student's best interest that the student, teacher, and parent work together. I will therefore be in close contact with parents regarding students' progress. Parents, please sign the tear off and have the student return it to me tomorrow. If you have any questions or comments, please call me or write them on the tear off.

After reviewing the rules with the students, I have them fill out a behavior card that becomes part of my system for recording behavior problems. This is yet another way of telling the students that discipline is an important part of my classroom organization. I begin by seating students according to a seating chart, then explain procedures concerning homework, grading, and required materials. Textbooks are distributed and we go over the plans for the semester. After that, we begin the first lesson. By the end of the first class, all students have the feeling that I am in control, with a well-organized plan.

Gradually over the years of trying various discipline approaches, I have found that students react positively to my system. As the year progresses, occasional gentle reminders are usually enough to maintain good behavior. I also use eye contact, hand signals, and physical proximity to assist. When more serious disruptions do occasionally occur, students know the rules and consequences and it thus becomes easier to invoke the consequences without emotional upheavals and confrontations that I find personally offensive.

High School System #2:

Teacher: Elaine Maltz
Subject: Math Basic Skills

At my first class meeting I distribute a copy of my class rules to each student. These are signed by parent and student and returned to me the next day. A copy of the rules is then kept in each student's math notebook.

The rules are as follows:

1. Come to class on time and be in your seat when the bell rings.
2. Bring your textbook, math notebook with paper, and a sharpened pencil every day.
3. Work quietly at your seat unless you have permission to do otherwise.
4. Food and drink are not allowed in the classroom.

Consequences: (all shown in citizenship grades)

- For tardiness: 0–3 tardies = G (good)
  4 tardies = S (satisfactory)
  5 tardies = N (needs improvement)
  6 tardies = U (unsatisfactory)
- For truancy: Two truancies lowers citizenship grade. Four truancies lowers academic grade.
- Infractions of other rules: 0–4 infractions = G
  5–6 infractions = S
  7–8 infractions = N
  9–10 infractions = U

When I present the rules, I discuss my expectations and explain the rules fully. I mention that in addition to my consequences, the school maintains a system by which students get referred to the counselor or vice principal. If necessary, the parents are contacted for assistance.

In teaching, I feel that an essential element of classes in math is the use of humor. It combats boredom as well as "math phobia." The tone has to be set at the beginning of the class, as a part of an overall atmosphere of acceptance and encouragement where each student is treated with respect. At the same time, the best is clearly expected of each student. I work hard to avoid sarcasm and try never to attack the students personally.

I find it also helps to provide occasional changes of pace. Reviewing homework, introducing new material, and starting corresponding homework are the nuts and bolts of my class, but I try to intersperse visual problems with abstract ones and include real problem solving at least once each class as a respite from routine work.

To help with behavior, I also stay active while my students are working at their seats, constantly circulating and helping. This not only allows me to help students with their work, but it permits me to deal subtly with incipient misbehavior without drawing the attention of other class members. I use eye contact, facial expressions, and light touches to help students control their own behavior.

I admit there are times when I use nagging, or the broken record technique, to remind students of standards and expectations. I do this to help my students give high priority to academics and to proper social behavior. At the same time, I remember to smile when dealing with my students. I think teenagers, more than others, need concrete proof of their teacher's feelings. Other ways I try to give this proof is to be as helpful as possible, get work corrected and back to students quickly, and provide nonending encouragement, especially to reluctant students. I work hard at all this. Being a consistent disciplinarian has not come naturally to me.

TWO INTERMEDIATE GRADE SYSTEMS

Intermediate Grade System #1:

Teacher: Nancy Natale

I believe a positive atmosphere is most conducive to learning, so I set up my discipline system so it will be fun and rewarding for my students. My system is based on points; the points have value that can later be used to buy items such as toys, games, and books.

Earning Points. Each student is able to earn points all during the week. I assign points for a number of different behaviors. For example, when I begin an activity I give points to those students who begin work immediately. First, I give them verbal praise: "Thank you, Jennifer; Good going, Shawn," and as I do this I give them each a point on a master chart I keep near my desk. This provides immediate reinforcement and also influences other students positively, reminding them that they too can earn points.

As an extra work incentive, I assign points to students who bring into class something that is pertinent to what we are studying. For example, one day I was teaching about diagrams. The next day a girl brought in a diagram of a house her parents were building and a boy brought in a diagram of a model airplane he was putting together.

I use discretion in offering numbers of points. For example, my class was writing autobiographies to be bound and displayed at open house but they just weren't using their time well. I decided to offer five points to each student who completed his or her work to my satisfaction by noon of the day of the open house. This motivated students to high work output.

I also give out points at unexpected times. In a recent geometry lesson we were discussing the number of faces, edges, and vertices that various shapes have. After we had examined about 10 different shapes, a girl pointed out to me that on every pyramid the number of faces was always equal to the number of vertices, regardless of whether the pyramid had a triangular, square, hexagonal, or other-shaped base. We tested her observation and found it to be true. I gave her a point for an excellent observation.

Class Rules. I use only four class rules. They are:

1. Pay attention during class.
2. Keep hands and feet to yourself.
3. Do not prevent others from learning.
4. Follow directions and complete your work.

Misbehavior. Even with all the attention I give to keeping a positive atmosphere, my students still misbehave sometimes. When they do, I have them fill out a "See Me" card. On this card the student must answer these four questions:

1. What was I doing?
2. Why was I doing it?
3. What should I have been doing?
4. What class rule was broken?

After the card is filled out, the student must bring it to me and we have a discussion about it. If any student accumulates three See Me cards in one week, that student has to write a letter to his or her parents stating why they received the cards. This procedure helps me document misbehaviors in my classroom, but better yet it makes the student take ownership of the misbehavior. If a student receives even one See Me card in a week, he or she may not participate in the week's spending of earned points, but must do homework instead.

Intermediate Grade System #2:

Teacher: Micheal Brus

I base my discipline system on the golden rule and find I need to spell out only three rules, which I prepare calligraphically in gold, Gothic lettering and display prominently in the room. My rules read as follows:

- Teachers have a right to teach;
- Students have a right to learn!

Therefore:

1. We agree to treat fellow students and teachers as we ourselves would like to be treated.
2. We agree to be on time, prepared to work, and to stay on task.
3. We agree to have no unauthorized food, gum, or drink.

I believe in treating my students very much like adults, letting them know they are responsible for how they behave. I define the behavior boundaries within my three rules and discuss gray areas around them. I invite my students to add a fourth rule, if there is one in which they believe strongly.

I use much positive reinforcement. Whenever I see a student behaving especially well, I ask him or her to go to the master list of student names (displayed on a wall chart) and make a vertical stroke beside the name with my gold marker. The student receiving the most marks in a month is named citizen of the month. Having been a professional portrait artist, I honor the student by drawing a color pastel portrait of him or her.

The points accumulated by other students may be used at an end-of-the-month auction to bid for prizes I furnish, such as inexpensive toys, books, erasers, pieces of chalk, and stickers. In order to emphasize good group behavior I keep a separate tally of points earned by the class as a whole for being quiet and orderly at lunch, library, auditorium, and especially for helping us all have an unusually pleasant day at school. These points accumulate toward free minutes on Fridays, extra physical education, or time for playing with computers and games.

By my own demeanor in the classroom I try to show my sincere belief that there is much good in every person. I try to find in all my students something they do especially well and help instill in them a sense of pride and achievement.

When my students break class rules, I have them go to the master chart and make a black tally mark beneath their name. The consequences associated with the black marks are as follows:

- First mark—I verbally reinforce the opposite behavior in another student.
- Second mark—I give a short verbal desist, referring to the rule that is broken.
- Third mark—I send the student to a fellow teacher's room, with an assignment to complete (this is arranged in advance, reciprocally, with the other teacher.
- Fourth mark—The student is sent to the principal's office. The principal knows and supports my system and takes further appropriate action.

When the consequences for more serious misbehavior are invoked, I follow up with the student, insisting that a plan for proper behavior be made that is acceptable to both the student and me. At appropriately private times, I talk openly and honestly with the student about his or her success in living up to the plan, and what must be done next when the plan does not work.

TWO PRIMARY LEVEL DISCIPLINE SYSTEMS

Primary System #1:

Teacher: Virginia Villalpando

The old proverb about an ounce of prevention being worth a pound of cure serves as the foundation for my discipline program. I arrange the environment so as to discourage misbehavior by arranging tables and chairs to allow easy access to instructional areas and provide clear lines of vision to all parts of the room. Supplies are placed in conveniently accessible locations. Special interest areas are separated from work areas so as not to distract students. I do not seat students closely together, and I make sure the seating allows me to reach every student in the room quickly when necessary.

I make my expectations known clearly on the first day. I emphasize that I want my students to have a learning environment that is free from disruptions, and that I will expect the students' help in keeping it friendly and pleasant. I let them know that I want to know their feelings, but that my decisions will be final. I go over the classroom rules, discuss what they mean, and explain the consequences for following and breaking them. I continually emphasize that behavior is their choice, as are the consequences of that behavior. I go over the rules, explain them with examples, and describe the consequences, as follows:

Rule	*Explanation*	*Consequence*
Respect others.	No hitting, tattling, name-calling. Let others work. Speak quietly, be kind.	Negative: time out, isolation, note to parents, stay in at recess. Positive: rewards.
Raise hand.	Do this before speaking, getting drink, asking for help, etc.	Negative: ignore, deny request, frown. Positive: praise, special reward, thanks.

Work quietly.	No loud noise; don't disturb others.	Positive: stars, smiley faces, thank-yous. Negative: move to other area.
Be orderly.	Don't run; enter room quietly; stay in line.	Positive: smile; praise. Negative: frown; checkmark by name on board.
Respect property.	Take care of things; keep them clean.	Positive: note home; thanks. Negative: note home.

I keep the basic rules (but not the explanations and consequences) posted on a chart at the front of the room. When students break the rules I invoke the consequences and often refer to the rules chart. If the infractions are minor or infrequent, I merely use eye contact or shakes of the head to get students back on track. I make a point of thanking them when they behave well. I smile and say "good, keep it up, that's the way." I want them to feel good about behaving well.

Primary Level System #2:

Teacher: Thomas F. Bolz

Two years ago I moved from teaching a fifth grade to a kindergarten-first grade combination. I soon learned a far different approach to discipline was required. Primary children get more excited about praise and correction—in fact, they get more excited about almost everything. At my school we have a discipline plan that everyone uses, but into that plan I weave much of my own philosophy and personality. The rules we all use are the following:

1. I will listen and follow directions.
2. I will respect and use kind words toward others. Profanity is not permitted.
3. I will keep hands, feet, and objects to myself. Fighting is prohibited.
4. I will complete all assigned work on time.
5. I will respect school property and the property of others.

These rules apply to the playground as well as to the classroom and school environment.

We have a hierarchy of consequences set up for students who break the rules. They are:

- Step 1. Verbal warning. Additional consequence if apology is necessary or if there is damage to property.
- Step 2. Conference with teacher, with one or more of the following results: repair of damage, time out, loss of recess, loss of a privilege.
- Step 3. Child remains after school and calls to notify parents of reason.
- Step 4. Teacher contacts parents to inform them of behavior and discuss consequences for the child. Teacher may set up conference with parents.
- Step 5. If all else fails and the child's behavior has not improved, teacher contacts the principal who decides on further consequences and sets up conference with parents.

Personally, I invest much time and energy into preventive and supportive discipline. When I want students to get in their seats, sitting up with hands folded, I give the direction and then start a nursery rhyme: "One, two, buckle my shoe. . ." Soon the whole class is reciting the rhyme, and by the time we get to "a big fat hen"—usually about 10 seconds—the whole class is attentive with their eyes on me.

Another preventive technique I use is the "good walker" tickets. Whenever we are walking down the hallway I hand out two or three tickets to students who are walking nicely. In class they put them in an oatmeal container and when we line up to go outside, I draw a ticket out. That person gets to be first in line.

The major breakthrough for the year has been the Happy Face Chart. Our day usually begins like this: "Elsie, Josh, and Aaron, boom! Sign the Happy Face. Notice how they came in quietly and sat up straight and tall." A tide of good behavior ripples out from that. At the end of the week, I read off the names for each day. The names are put on slips of paper for a drawing. Whoever wins gets a coupon for a bag of french fries.

When it comes to corrective discipline, I want it to be short, simple, clearly understood, and unpleasant for the child. When individual children are noisy or not doing their work I have them put their head down at their desk. Children know that they then have to count to 100 by ones, think about what they were doing wrong, and then get back to work. If I have to speak to them again during the day, they go to the time-out chair where I have a 3-minute egg timer. They have to sit for that length of time. They understand that this is a severe warning. The third time I have to talk with them I put their name on the board with a check and call their parent. This corrects the behavior most of the time.

I am able to enforce these rules most of the time without getting upset. I make sure the children know I expect them to behave better. One parent commented to me that her daughter liked my room because I was "fair and treated everyone alike."

TWO SPECIALTY SYSTEMS

Specialty System #1: Behavior Modification

Teacher: Constance Bauer

I had been teaching for 5 or 6 years before I ever understood what behavior modification was all about and what it could do for teachers. I had controlled my second graders through the usual stern-voiced admonitions, and had tried to motivate them by telling them how much fun we were going to have in school that day. Neither approach ever went over quite well enough to suit me.

Then, our school had an inservice training session on behavior modification and its uses in the classroom. Because our principal expected us to, I half-heartedly began to try out some of the approaches in my classroom— such things as finding a student who was behaving correctly and praising that behavior rather than scolding those who were misbehaving, and setting up a "bookworm" chart so that students who did their work could add another segment to their worm.

My students responded so well to those first efforts that I decided to see what more I could accomplish with positive reinforcement. I set up individual progress charts for my students so they could keep track of their improvement in reading, math, and spelling. I made little stuffed rabbits that could sit on desks where there were "good workers." I made note forms that I sent home each day with "good helper" students, so their parents could be proud of them.

Before long I found that I was controlling and motivating the class with these devices and everything was going much more smoothly and positively than ever before. I am told that it is easier to use such programs at the primary grade level than with older students. I don't know if that's so, but in any case behavior modification has made a believer out of me.

Specialty System #2: Token Economy

Teachers: Mike Straus and Roy Allen (team teachers)

For the first few years we taught, we used authority as our way of keeping discipline. We are large and can talk mean and order students to behave.

But that was wearing us out and making the kids afraid of us. Nobody was enjoying school very much.

Then one year we decided to try a behavior control system based on fake money. We called our currency "Strallens" (our names combined), and we printed up several hundred bills of different denominations. A couple of years ago a student's mother took photographs of us and made up a batch of Strallens with our pictures on them.

Anyway, we decided to pay our students Strallens when they worked quietly, did their homework, finished work on time, did extra work, participated well in class, and so on. We also decided we would fine them when they didn't do their work or misbehaved or talked back. We have heard that in behavior modification you give rewards for good behavior, but don't do anything when the kids act bad. That's not real life, so far as we are concerned. In society when you break the law you get fined, and that was how we wanted it in our classroom.

We usually walk around the classroom with Strallens in our hand or pocket. We give them out personally. When students misbehave, like talking when they're not supposed to, we say "Jack, that's a 10 Strallen fine." Jack knows he has to go put 10 of his Strallens in the fine box.

As students accumulate Strallens, they can use them to buy special things we provide. Every couple of weeks, for example, we rent a video movie that the kids want to see. We charge admission. Those who don't have enough Strallens can't watch the movie. We have popcorn sometimes and field trips to interesting places and white elephant sales. Students can spend Strallens for those things, too.

After a while some of the students don't care to spend their Strallens —they want to see how many they can get. Some amass several hundred. We set up bank accounts, too, that earn interest, to teach students about interest, writing checks, and balancing check books.

Our system has worked for us. We almost never have to scold a student. They accept the rewards and fines as reasonable and everyone stays in a pretty good mood most of the time.

The Strallen system doesn't work for every student. We tell students at the beginning that they don't have to participate in it if they don't want to. They can have the usual praise if they behave and the usual scoldings and staying-in if they don't. An occasional student takes that option. Once in a while a student on the Strallen system misbehaves so much they go hopelessly in the hole. We take them off the system and use conventional controls with them.

All in all, we like our system. It is effective, easy to operate, and the kids react to it positively. It has made our teaching easier and more enjoyable.

Index